T0360484

Gold Standard Sustainability Reporting

This highly practical and concise book shows you how to undertake a reporting process and produce a sustainability report in line with the new standards and frameworks presented by the International Integrated Reporting Council (IIRC) and the Global Reporting Initiative (GRI). Fully updated to ensure compliance with the new standards, this second edition shows how to actually produce a sustainability report as well as the key processes in the planning: how to produce a business case; the development of actions plans; process and team leadership; and generating cross-functional buy-in. Templates are provided for certain steps in order to simplify the tasks involved at each point in the process. Anyone involved in delivering or developing a process to embed sustainability reporting for an organisation will find this book invaluable, for example, chief sustainability officers, chief financial officers and company secretaries. It will also be of interest to students in the field of sustainability.

Kye Gbangbola is the founder of Total Eco Management (TEM), a sustainability consultancy providing a variety of sustainability strategy, management and reporting tools and services.

Nicole Lawler is Global Director of Sustainability at Total Eco Management (TEM).

Gold Standard Sustainability Reporting

A Step by Step Guide to Producing
a Sustainability Report

Second Edition

Kye Gbangbola and Nicole Lawler

LONDON AND NEW YORK

Second edition published 2020
by Routledge
2 Park Square, Milton Park, Abingdon, Oxon, OX14 4RN

and by Routledge
52 Vanderbilt Avenue, New York, NY 10017

Routledge is an imprint of the Taylor & Francis Group, an informa business

© 2020 Kye Gbangbola and Nicole Lawler

First edition published by Greenleaf 2014

British Library Cataloguing-in-Publication Data
A catalogue record for this book is available from the British Library

Library of Congress Cataloging-in-Publication Data
A catalog record for this book has been requested

ISBN: 978-0-367-34588-4 (hbk)
ISBN: 978-1-003-01168-2 (ebk)

Typeset in Times New Roman
by Apex CoVantage, LLC

This book is dedicated to the memory of our beautiful son, Zane Gbangbola, an angelic figure on earth who passed in God's grace; a happy, happy boy who lived surrounded in love and exuded it back tenfold.

The story of Zane is that the world was a much richer place with him in it. We know this because of the many children, family, friends, engineering and speed icons, teachers, trainers, neighbours, communities, executives and so on who hold fond, happy memories of him and who miss him so very much.

Our God mourns with us at the passing of our son and journeys alongside us knowing how proud we are to be Zane's parents and to have learnt so much from Zane, who was the St. George's School Eco Team Founder member, enthusiastic to make the world a better place, where everybody takes their responsibility seriously as custodians to nurture the world for future generations.

Zane's approach to sustatainability was visionary for a child, as he asked his Head Teacher, for whom he had huge regard and respect, about setting up a green team to respond to the world, children, and people in need locally and globally. One of Zane's acts that came to light was a request he made that the school no longer use helium ballons on Ascension Day; he knew that helium is a natural gas to be preserved. It was five years later when children across the world would rise up and implore adults and parliaments in their countries to change rapidly to establish a sustainable world, abate the crisis of extinction and climate change, and turn to a world of renewables, restoration and global protection from those waging war on the planet and polluting it with waste. Zane would have certainly been an instigator on the front line alongside Greta Thunburg, Extinction Rebellion and David Attenborough, and, as parents, we would be proud to back him.

Zane is Hebrew for 'Gift from God'. Thank you for truly beautiful, fantastic and wonderful times and for the love you showed to everybody.

Richard, Andy, Zane, Joe and the Team, all the best at Hakskeen.

A few words of thanks to the TEM Team, GRI, Routledge and a dedication to all children who themselves aspire to a better world for their children in the quest for global change!

'Even the smallest person can change the course of the future'.

Contents

Diagrams, templates and schedules   x
Abstract   xi
About the authors   xiii
Disclaimer   xv
Feedback   xvi
Who this book is for   xvii
About this book   xix
Foreword   xxii
Preface   xxiv

Introduction to sustainability reporting   1

1 Sustainability context   4
The journey 4
Sustainable Development Goals 7
Preliminaries 8
Preparing the business case – board approval 12
Setting out 17

2 Prepare   20
Assembling the team 20
*Understanding the GRI Standards and choosing the 'in
    accordance' option 21*
Development Plan 24
*Kick-off meeting (agreement on the reporting process)
    and engaging internal stakeholders 25*

3 Connect (wide range of stakeholders) 28
Identify stakeholders 29
Prioritise stakeholders 30
Stakeholder engagement 31
Build stakeholder relationships 37

4 Define 38
Determine the material topics 40
Produce materiality matrix and determine 'thresholds' 42
Validate material topics 43

5 Monitor 45
Monitor topics and set policies and procedures to measure
*   as necessary 47*
Set SMART goals and targets 49

6 Report 52
Develop narrative for most senior person's statement 56
Company accreditations 56
The Declaration 57
Draft sustainability/integrated report 57
Content index 57
Omissions 61
GRI report-checking services 61
Finalise report and send for publication 63
Launch report 63
Feedback 64

7 Software 65

8 Assurance 67

9 Additional insights for reporters and non-reporters 70
Integrated reporting 70

10 Q&A for reporters and non-reporters 74

11 Sustainability report evaluation 77

**Appendix 1 The usual suspects – an idea of material topics
        and challenges for organisations in different sectors** 86

Glossary 89
Bibliography 98
Index 100

Diagrams, templates and schedules

Diagram 1	GRI Sustainability Reporting Process	xx
Diagram 2	Selection of Sustainability Reports	2
Diagram 3	GRI Sustainability Reporting Process	17
Diagram 4	Stakeholders That Affect an Organisation – Identification	30
Diagram 5	Stakeholder Groups Engaged, How Consulted, and How Often	33
Diagram 6	Overview of Process for Defining Report Content and Boundary	39
Diagram 7	Materiality Scatter Matrix	42
Schedule 1	Sustainability Reporting Timeline	9
Schedule 2	Prepare Phase Timeline	20
Schedule 3	Connect Phase Timeline	28
Schedule 4	Define Phase Timeline	38
Schedule 5	Monitor Phase Timeline	46
Schedule 6	Report Phase Timeline	53
Table 2.1	GRI In Accordance Option Disclosures	23
Table 2.2	Categories and Topics in the GRI Standards	26
Table 3.1	Stakeholder Prioritisation	32
Table 5.1	Data Collection and Monitoring	48
Table 5.2	SMART Targets	50
Template 1	Board Report Business Case for Sustainability Reporting	12
Template 2	Kick-off Meeting Agenda	27
Template 3	Stakeholder Engagement	33
Template 4	Sustainability Report Contents Table	54
Template 5	Content Index	59

Abstract

Corporate reporting in the form of environmental social governance has a few commonly used names; it is part of Corporate Social Responsibility (CSR), which we call 'Common Sense Really'. Other names include sustainability reporting or integrated reporting. For many involved in the management and leadership of organisations these are interchangable and increasingly business critical activities undertaken by larger companies and their supply chains. The worlds most commonly used reporting instrument standard is the Global Reporting Initiative Standards, known as the GRI Standards. In some countries up to 90% of organisations that report do so to the GRI Standards. It is ideal as a pathway to generating all types of CSR/ sustainability reports.

This book is a step-by-step guide to the practices and processes to produce a sustainability report. This guide is also for stakeholders, investors and asset managers; indeed, anyone who wants to evaluate reports. The book will answer your questions about how any part of the reporting process is carried out, including templates, documents and methodologies, so you can save time and money by not having to reinvent the wheel to get started or improve your reporting.

This is not a book on what the GRI Standards are all about, as the six modules comprising the GRI Universal Standards and the Topic Specific Standards do that admirably; indeed our consultancy, Total Eco Management, offers a globally renowned and awarded GRI Masterclass to executives and post-graduates from around the world on the GRI Standards.

This book is about the journey an organisation can use to deliver a quality corporate sustainability report in response to the many reporting instruments, of which GRI represents the gold standard. The content and quality of a sustainability report distinguishes the reporter; it should be concise, focused on the material topics and tell the story of how strategy, governance, performance and prospects lead to the creation and preservation of short, medium and long-term business value.

This is a self-help book and the first book that shows how to actually produce a sustainability report and the journey surrounding and deciding on the public commitments made. If we are serious about moving to a sustainable world, we need to become sustainability literate.

About the authors

Kye Gbangbola, MBA, is the founder and **Nicole Lawler** is the Global Director of Sustainability at Total Eco Management (TEM), a sustainability consultancy providing a variety of sustainability strategy, management and reporting tools and services. Kye and Nicole are passionate about sustainability in all of its guises, especially corporate management and behaviours for long-term resilience and leadership. Many refer to them as 'game changers' because they inspire and challenge.

TEM was the first Global Reporting Initiative (GRI)-certified training provider in the United Kingdom and Republic of Ireland and the first GRI-certified partner to deliver a GRI-approved GRI training programme in the UK. It provides the first GRI-certified training course to be accredited by the Institute of Environmental Management & Assessment (IEMA), of which Kye is a fellow, as well as being registered on GRI's exclusive global list of GRI experts. Kye is also a GACSO (Global Association of Corporate Sustainability Officer) member, sustainability ambassador to the Chartered Institute of Building, where he is a fellow, and he was a domestic energy assessor.

Kye and Nicole are the authors of many blogs and articles on topics including sustainability, assurance, integrated reporting, sustainability equality and disability, energy generation, measuring up to the carbon challenge, life cycle analysis, sustainable construction, leadership, climate change, conflict minerals, biodiversity, materiality, GRI measurement and reporting, and many others.

Disclaimer

This is not an official publication of the Global Reporting Initiative, and its content has not been reviewed by any member of the GRI in any official capacity. This book is entirely the work of the authors, who as GRI-certified training partners, and on the global list of GRI experts, have a detailed understanding of the GRI Standards. The authors do not accept liability for future changes to the GRI Standards guidance, which may affect the guidance provided in this book.

All GRI publications mentioned in this book relating to the GRI Standards Guidelines can be found and freely downloaded via the GRI website: www.globalreporting.org.

Feedback

We appreciate your feedback and comments.

Main Line: +44 (0) 1932 567002
Email: info@temltd.co.uk

Who this book is for

This book is relevant to any organisation or body that wants to know how to write a sustainability report and understand how its constituent parts are developed. It also enables stakeholders who have a professional, personal or academic interest in reporting to learn how to evaluate a report, which is also an essential skill for report writers.

This book provides practical and compact information delivered quickly and efficiently so that organisations can appreciate that the communication of these corporate documents needs to be concise in the delivery of high-quality information for management and stakeholders.

This book is for you if:

- You are experienced in GRI reporting and want to use the GRI Standards.
- You are new to sustainability reporting.
- You understand the value of transparency and want to formalise existing good sustainability practices at your organisation into a recognised standard.
- You are a large company reporting to the GRI G4 and seek easy transition to GRI Standards reporting.
- You are at the start of, or considering, the sustainability journey.
- You want to employ sustainability professionals and want to understand what the role entails so that you can seek the best person for the job.
- You want to consider/compare GRI Standards alongside other standards used by your company or its sector.
- You are an SME or private company seeking the benefits that investing in sustainability brings, including greater access to work, greater stakeholder trust, reputation and loyalty, higher income, reduced expenditures, and so on.

- You want to align the leadership, staff and stakeholders on how to report and dispell confusion on understanding and awareness of the process and outcomes.
- You simply seek to cultivate or nurture an interest for academic continuous professional development reasons.
- You, as a stakeholder, want to understand what is involved when a company reports, explains and discloses sustainability issues.
- You, as a stakeholder or investor, seek the knowledge to evaluate GRI Standards reports.

Organisations have an opportunity to show they are part of the solution through their corporate sustainability reporting. Organisations need to frame their sustainability thinking in an orderly, relevant and transparent manner; this is precisely what good sustainability reporting provides. To be clear, failure affects reputation, but bigger than that, contributing to harming the planet is becoming unacceptable when there is so much that can be done to contribute to change.

About this book

This is a how-to book, enabling individuals and organisations to reap the rewards of sustainability reporting. The book can be used to change an organisation for the greater good, for both the organisation and society, meeting Sustainable Development Goal requirements. Organisations know they need to report so as to provide evidence of their journey of change, and this book shows you how this is done.

The book shows the reader how to produce a business case, develop action plans, secure leadership over the process and people and generate cross-functional buy-in. It shows you the basics of how to prepare an organisation for reporting, how to do stakeholder engagement, how to do materiality, how to collect quality data, how to do assurance, how to plan, write and structure the report, how to apply and manage GRI's own report-checking services, how to finalise and disseminate a report and then position it on media platforms for dissemination and feedback. These are the things organisations need and want to know to improve the quality of their reporting processes.

This book is a step-by-step guide to the practices and processes needed to produce a sustainability/integrated report. The book itself is structured around the GRI sustainability reporting process (Diagram 1).

It is not GRI's (or any reporting instrument's) job to detail day-to-day operational approaches for report production. GRI produces and promotes the framework, guidance and disclosure requirements. This book provides the means to deliver a sustainability report that should meet the requirements of GRI and other standards and frameworks. However, it is our view that an organisation doing GRI well will meet the IIRC requirements anyway, so we have placed the emphasis on doing the GRI Standards well.

Whatever standards you choose, remember that your report is not just about you, but it is more about how your actions affect the rest of us and the planet. Many stakeholders do not even know they are stakeholders; they do not know they are impacted by your actions, know little about you, do not

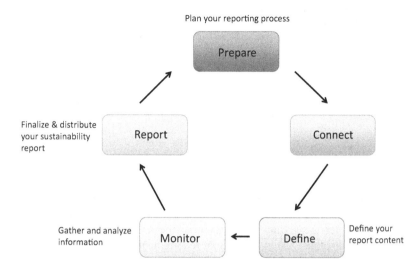

Diagram 1 GRI Sustainability Reporting Process

read your report and have no interest in your financial well-being like investors do. So it means that your material issues, which are determined by your impacts, must be measured against authoritative international standards of behaviour; they must be measured against the expectations created not by a company's management, but by others as to what constitutes responsible business behaviour, and they must be motivated by a sense of what is right and wrong. GRI and other standards provide the international recognition of robust corporate thinking for the good of people, planet and profit.

As experts, we, the authors, have worked with companies and their supply chains to improve their reporting. We will lead you by the hand through the concepts and end with a handy report evaluation tool as we do in our Sustainability Reporting Masterclass.

This book is designed with you in mind. This book is the equivalent to having an expert on hand when you need them, giving you access 24/7/365.

This book is relevant to any type of sustainability reporter, not just GRI. It also explains the value of reporting and does not over-indulge in the socio-political argument. This book takes you onto the field of play where every supporter, fan and observer would prefer to be if only they knew how, and that's worth paying for.

Many readers of this book will have already looked through the GRI Standards and other frameworks and guidelines and been frustrated because they need to understand how to apply it to their situation. Well, now you can by using this book.

We have come across people who argue that such frameworks are a distraction, that they do not enable organisations to focus on reducing environmental impact or improving social impact. However, not having a framework leaves a company and its advisors to 'make it up' as they go along. It is important not to be distracted from the use of international norms because it is these norms that provide the structure and operational approaches needed for stakeholders and experts to have 'trust'. Action on impacts needs authoritative international standards of behaviour motivated by a sense of what is right and wrong, and this is undoubtedly what some frameworks provide. Having a map so that one does not become lost on the journey, as this book provides, simply makes the journey easier and can help make visible the least line of resistance. It can help answer the many questions arising on the reporting journey. For some it may even stop the rat in the kitchen from letting the others in.

Foreword

We have entered into what might be called the Age of Transparency. Driven and facilitated by technology and instant access to information, we have arrived in the 'show me' society where, if claims are to be believed, they must be backed by trustworthy information.

This has occurred at the same time as several critical sustainability trends have taken on what many see as emergency status. The build-up of greenhouse gases in the atmosphere, depletion of certain natural resources and loss of biological diversity are among them.

Not only are these topics of environmental change already challenging to manage, but they are expected to get worse as continuing population and economic growth place yet more demand on the finite base of ecological capacity that enables our world to function. This is everybody's problem, and not only because of the ethical questions raised but also because of the new spread of risks that are emerging.

Whereas businesses once treated the environmental impacts they caused as a threat to their reputation, the hazards that are emerging alongside deteriorating ecological services are far bigger. Disruption caused by extreme weather, price volatility arising from resource scarcity and supply chain disruption, linked with the degradation of environmental services, are already evident and already impacting companies.

So, what can be done in this new and fast-changing situation? One thing is to gather high-quality and relevant information, organise it in sensible ways and then disseminate it so that different user communities can benefit from it. And that, in a nutshell, is what this book is all about: how best to gather and present sustainability information so that it can have maximum beneficial impact, both inside companies and among their stakeholders.

The proportion of companies producing decent sustainability reports has grown fast in recent years and, as a result, it is now possible to see some of the benefits that come with this.

One is to improve business-to-business relationships, as companies in each other's supply chains increasingly select partners based upon their commitment and performance in relation to various environmental and sustainability questions. Another benefit can be seen in relation to more effective risk management and how those companies with better information are more able to understand and anticipate business drivers, including unpredictable and volatile ones. This is now beginning to be reflected in companies' financial performance and is thus of great interest to investors.

And as more experience is gained through better reporting, so the front line of good practice moves forward. Today it is no longer sufficient to present separate information on the environment, social issues and financial performance, with simple trade-offs and a 'balance' implied between them.

It is, by contrast, now increasingly necessary to take truly integrated approaches, not least in the context of the ever more widely expressed goal of achieving a 'net positive impact'. To be credible in making progress towards that stretching goal requires many tools, not least credible information presented in compelling ways.

To unlock this constellation of opportunity it is important to gather, organise and disseminate information in ways that press multiple buttons. By reading this short and easy-to-use guide, you can find out how to do that, and in the process gain maximum value from sustainability reporting. I hope a great many people will read it and, through better understanding the impacts of what they are doing, be in a position to better manage the risks facing both their company and society at large.

DR TONY JUNIPER
Co-founder, Robertsbridge Group, Fellow with the University of
Cambridge Institute for Sustainability Leadership and President of the
Society for the Environment
W: www.tonyjuniper.com
T: @tonyjuniper

Preface

This is a self-help book enabling individuals and organisations to reap the rewards of reporting. The book can be used to change an organisation for the greater good of both the organisation and society and to become part of the growing global phenomenon for a sustainable world. Organisations know they need to report as the vehicle to evidence of their journey of change, and this book shows you how this is done.

The book is balanced, providing positive and negative topics as appropriate whilst being constructive as to how organisations can maximise the opportunity reporting offers to them, being increasingly 'net positive' in their impacts. This point is made so there is no confusion that it offers constructive views, not dogma and devotion that is candy-coated for a topic or soured against a topic.

Introduction to sustainability reporting

This short section on sustainability reporting is to get you tuned in to what sustainability reporting is all about. We will look at the definition of sustainability reporting, then consider the latest positions in the reporting environment and wrap up the section with what needs to change.

Let's tell it straight. We are amidst a global sustainability and climate crisisrecently called out by the likes of Greta Thunberg, Extinction Rebellion and Sir David Attenborough. Politicians are being implored to recognise the truth of what is happening and respond to save people and species here and around the world. At issue is attitude; when will people and the powerful become invested in the need to change?

Recognition of the climate emergency by governments would engage governments and organisations in framing their sustainability credentials. This book shows organisations how to use the tool of sustainability reporting well, to underpin the eroding foundations of life and move to sustainable economies.

The United Nations (UN) states that around 1 million animals and plants are threatened with extinction. Ten percent of the world's insect species and 33% of marine mammals are threatened. The UN says that the record rate of species decline will continue unless world leaders take urgent action to combat climate change, pollution and land use.

Some organisations interchange their reporting terms between Corporate Responsibility or Corporate Social Responsbility and sustainability reporting; for the purposes of this book we will be using the term 'sustainability reporting' to cover all the terms.

A sustainability report is a public report about an organisation's social, environmental, economic and social impacts of its day-to-day activities, and hence its positive and negative contributions towards the goal of a sustainable global economy.

A sustainability report is the result of a sustainability reporting process. The reporting process is the practice of measuring, disclosing and being accountable to internal and external stakeholders for the economic,

Diagram 2 Selection of Sustainability Reports

environmental and social impacts caused by the organisation through its everyday activities.

A report should reflect the magnitude of contribution and impact of an organisation and be balanced; for this reason and several more rewarding ones, reporting is suitable for organisations of all types, sizes and sectors as a means of understanding how to create and sustain short, medium and long-term value. KPMG reports a strong correlation between reporting and increased returns for investors and support for the objectives of Agenda 2030, the UN Sustainable Development Goals.

KPMG's Survey on Corporate Reporting 2017 surveyed over 4,900 companies, comprising the top 100 companies by revenue in each of the 49 countries surveyed. It confirms that sustainability reporting is now standard practice for large and mid-cap companies around the world, over two-thirds of whom report, but 95% of the G250 report. However, there are some serious consistency and quality-of-reporting issues, especially revolving around materiality, which only a small minority do well. KPMG was also concerned with the areas of stakeholder engagement, balanced reports, use of performance measures and topics, data collection, the setting of targets and assurance. KPMG says more reporting regulations are coming; this is understandable as stakeholders increasingly demand better quality reporting.

The emphasis in reporting has also shifted from 'whether or not' to report, to 'at what quality' to report, and this forms another reason for producing this book. The survey found that more and more organisations are reporting voluntarily; however, the introduction of reporting regulations by over 55 governments and 44 stock exchanges is further driving forward sustainability reporting. KPMG states that reporting integration (i.e. economic, social and environmental; non-financial reporting) is the new financial. Indeed, in Denmark, France and South Africa, regulation has resulted in almost 100% reporting rates, and Kye's country of origin, Nigeria, is pointed out by KPMG as having high rates. The European Non-Financial Reporting Directive (requiring large companies to disclose social, environmental and diversity information) is set to increase still further the already high rates across Europe; it will have full effect in 2020.

Critics of reporting, who say it is too expensive with no return, that it is smoke and mirrors and insincerity, or that it is too complex, have been left behind. KPMG is clear that organisations not reporting are unlikely to remain in business. It is now understood that, for those who do reporting properly, the rewards are considerable, ranging from improved reputation, income, profit, share price, staff retention, credibility and reduced costs and recognition. (M&S's report has won over 240 awards, as identified in their 2017 report.)

Yes, sustainability reporting, done properly, requires financial and human resources, but so does any form of reporting, and an integrated report can cut considerable publication costs. The Dow Jones Group found that over a five-year period, the Group Sustainability Index performed at an average of 36.1% better than did the traditional Dow Jones Group Index.

A sustainability report should be a disciplined corporate document. Any stakeholder should be able to pick one up and know what its content will be. It should be a concise accurate and quality document and should also be compelling and clear on where the organisation creates value.

KPMG points out that the process can be poor and that organisations need more help. This is precisely what the book aims to deliver to overcome reporting quality issues, but it additionally enables new reporters to engage, and provides tools for stakeholders, investors and analysts to evaluate sustainability reports.

In our daily work with organisations, we offer them our top tips; an important one to remember is that a sustainability report is an output, while the real driver is an organisation's values, key capitals and business model as regards how the organisation delivers changes in its performance towards a sustainable global economy.

Bloomberg, M&S, GRI, Nike, CO-Op, Ferrari, CRH, WBA, several of these we trained

1 Sustainability context

The need and demand for change has made sustainability reporting a critical success factor in business. The Global Green Economy in 2016 was estimated at $7.87 trillion, according to University College London in 2019. The value associated with sustainabilty to meet the Sustainable Development Goals is estimated as needing to be $12 trillion per annum. The sustainability sector has been growing at an annual rate of 22% per annum since 2003 (International Finance Corporation World Bank Group). It is clear that green and sustainable economies are growing in significance relative to the world's combined wealth of $241 trillion.

Reporting using the GRI framework is applicable in every country in the world. It enables an organisation to anticipate regulation coming down the line, to participate in and to contribute to sustainable global economies.

Sustainability reporting requires a systematic approach to the processes involved. To work well it needs board and executive 'buy-in'. When the department that drives sustainability reporting does not have a mandate to set a strategy for the company or influence other departments' goals, programs and priorities, it is often reflected in the quality of the reporting.

This book reflects and respects that present and future generations across the world are at risk of starvation and thirst as hundreds of years of industrialisation pushes nature's safety net towards the breaking point, including millions of plant and animal species becoming extinct. This is the message from the UN, World Wildlife Fund, Intergovernmental Climate Change Panel and a sustainability report showing how an organisation contributes to safeguarding the planet and the preservation of humanity.

The journey

It is useful to frame the reporting journey in terms of the four principles of GRI reporting: sustainability context, stakeholder inclusivity, materiality and completeness (SIMC). It should be noted that this terminology is taken from the language of accounting. This is deliberate because sustainability reporting is simply an evolved form of corporate management accounts. Whereas once the financial accounts told us 100% of what we needed to know about the well-being of a company, it now only represents 20% of the information needs of stakeholders, with investors, for instance, needing information on the social, environmental and economic performance to appreciate the short, medium and long-term prospects of an organisation.

A sustainability report sets out the organisation's vision and intent; it states what environmental, social, governance and economic topics are relevant to the organisation and its stakeholders, and the activities to improve performance in these areas. The common metrics used enable reporting organisations to be assured and ranked based on quality.

The journey to develop the actual report begins with understanding this 'sustainability context'. The organisation should be able to present its performance in the wider context of sustainability issues. This involves an appreciation of and discussion on the limits and demands placed on environmental or social resources at the sector, local, regional and global levels.

Climate Change – Anthropogenic emissions contributing to sea level rise, degradation of biodiversity and endangering food and water resources. The International Energy Agency (IEA) cites that global energy-related carbon emissions increased by 1.4% on 2011 levels to a record 31.6 billion tonnes. Energy use has nudged above the danger zone of 400ppm; in April 2013 it was 399.72ppm. In the meantime, extreme weather-related insurance claims have increased 350% in Canada in the last two years (2012, 2013), and 64% of UK businesses have suffered supply chain disruption. The UK has a National Adaptation Programme (NAP) which models climate adaptation and is a sector worth £65.8 billion worldwide. The cost of the 2007 UK floods was estimated at £3.2 billion, the 2014 floods at £14.5 million, yet the cost of adaptation necessary to avert floods is estimated at a quarter of the cost of making good. Flood waters are killing people by toxic gas release. A one-degree temperature rise on earth is likely to generate low maize production for 60% of growers and have negative impacts on food chains and ecosystems.

Last year the World Bank reported that economic losses from extreme weather events have risen from an annual global average of about £31 billion in the 1980s to close to £124 billion over the last decade.

Water – Aquifers and water courses are being polluted and scarce potable supplies are diminishing. Water is essential to health and sanitation, but the Millennium Development Goals to provide basic sanitation to 1 billion people were not achieved.

Waste – The hierarchy is 1 Prevention, 2 Reuse, 3 Recycling, 4 Recovery, 5 Disposal. Government policy in the UK and increasingly globally seeks a circular economy, a closed loop from cradle to cradle. Japan is the number one circular economy, spending 7% of GDP in a £163 billion PA industry employing 650,000 people. China and the USA are similar, but sadly, the UK is outside the top ten for research (Circular Economy Taskforce Report 2013). Waste to Energy best practice includes recycling, composting, reusing metals and generating fuel. But increasingly, Waste to Energy is giving way to valorisation, which takes the constituent parts of waste into processes that manufacture new products within circular economies.

Increasingly, waste going to landfills is being rejected, not least because it stores up problems for future generations, but also it can pollute local communities through several pathways that harm the health of people and species by bio-accumulation.

Wealth Distribution – 85% of global wealth belongs to the richest 10%, the poorest half of the world's population owns 1% of global wealth, and the gap between rich and poor continues to grow. Four hundred million Africans earn less than $1.29 a day. Winnie Byanyima of Oxfam commented at the World Economic Forum on their report 'Working for the Few', which discusses how the current model of growth leaves people behind by driving inequality and public instability. This can't be moral. In 2014, 85 people owned half of the global wealth, but by 2018 this was down to 8 people owning half of the global wealth. Such financial wealth enables the hijacking of political power and the elite capture of law-making. Sustainability can enable and build different models so that growth is not a race to the bottom.

Population – Global population is 7.5 billion people and rising, placing greater pressure on resources; the last two years' growth is equivalent to twice the population of Holland.

Conservation – This is the need to preserve natural ecosystems and the environment.

Pollution – Toxic chemicals in the air and sea (i.e. atmospheric aerosol loading and chemical pollution, including radioactive compounds, heavy metals and organic compounds). Singapore recently had particulate levels ten times higher than the exposure guidelines set out by the World Health Organisation (WHO) due to smog caused by the burning of forests in Indonesia.

Once an organisation appreciates its sustainability context, it is able to have more meaningful and strategic dialogue with its stakeholders. This is the requirement of 'inclusivity': the need to identify and engage very carefully as stakeholders who will identify the topics selected as 'material'.

'Completeness' relates to the ability of the organisation to command and control the material topics based on the boundaries identified. It will be the impacts arising from these that enable stakeholders to assess an organisation's performance.

The acronym I call 'CRAB TC' governs quality, which is also quasi accountancy speak.

Clarity means readers should be able to understand the report and its contents.

Reliability means the information can be laid out so that it can be checked.

Accuracy means data should be accurate and capable of being checked and reproduction used to achieve similar results.

Balance means the report should be an unbiased picture of the organisation's performance.

Timeliness means publishing on a consistent schedule.

Comparability means information is comparable to past performance years and, if possible, to other organisations.

Sustainable Development Goals

The Sustainable Development Goals (SDGs) were formulated by the United Nations in 2015 under the 2030 Agenda for Sustainable Development. As a group, the SDGs provide a long-term North Star to guide businesses in value creation.

There are 17 goals over 169 targets to be delivered by 2030. The goals are targeted to end poverty, protect the planet and ensure prosperity for all as part of a new global sustainable development agenda. Each goal has specific targets to be achieved over the next 15 years.

The challenge for businesses is to come through with meaningful contributions to the global effort to achieve the SDGs. Organisations must appreciate their purpose relative to outward global, regional and local sustainability issues. Despite the short period of time since SDGs were introduced, the Chief Executive statements in GRI Standard reports refer to the goals; KPMG's 2017 survey states that 43% (and rapidly rising) Fortune 500 G250s incorporate SDGs in their reporting.

Reporting is the link between big-picture ambitions and the data that shows action has been taken to achieve these ambitions and what progress is being made. Without reporting, we cannot see what is being done or how close or how far we are from where the world needs to be. Indeed, the SDGs include a specific goal: 12.6 to encourage companies to integrate sustainability information into their reporting cycles.

GRI is the ideal standard to use when incorporating the goals; indeed, GRI has a memorandum of understanding (MOU) with the UN aligning

GRI and UN metrics of disclosure. GRI have similar MOUs with other standards bodies, such as the Carbon Disclosure Project, the International Standards Organisation, the UN Global Compact, the UN Principles of Business, the Organisation for Economic Cooperation and Development Multinational Enterprise Guidelines. So, by using GRI, organisations can respond to numerous other standards without the need for conversion formulae. GRI's mutual standard recognition is a powerful platform that all main standards bodies recognise as a major advantage to organisations that issue corporate reports to the GRI Standards.

Preliminaries

Sustainability leader and coordinator

This is the person in the organisation responsible for coordinating sustainability performance targets and sustainability report production. Ideally, the chief executive or chief sustainability officer is the sustainability leader, and if they are unable to do it themselves, they manage a member of staff with day-to-day responsibility for organising, coordinating and making sure that the sustainability reporting process is established, implemented and maintained and that documentation is produced in between meetings. The sustainability leader does not need to be an expert in environmental issues. It is more important that they understand organisational culture, structure and operations, and that they have good networking and project management skills.

An Eco Team comprising representatives from the functional departments should meet periodically to manage progress against targets and ensure that staff are participating in the process by attending workshops and taking follow-up action as necessary. Senior management and decision makers should constantly be involved and meet especially at the kick-off meeting and materiality validation that determines which topics are the highest priority for the organisation to carry forward to the Monitor phase of the reporting cycle (more on the kick-off meeting and materiality in the following chapters). Regular review meetings should assess opportunities for improvement, SMART methods of data/information collection, objectives and targets, monitoring, follow-up on previous sustainability reports and meeting actions, and corrective actions, audits and so on. These should all be noted and recorded. Schedule 1 provides the complete timeline and the activities the sustainability leader must ensure are managed.

Schedule 1 Sustainability Reporting Timeline

INDICATIVE SUSTAINABILITY REPORTING PROCESS ('POST BUSINESS CASE AND BOARD APPROVAL TO REPORT')

	April	May	June	July	August	September	October	November	December	January	February	March	April	May	June	July	August	September
	1 8 15 22 29	5 12 19 26	3 10 17 24	7 14 21 28	4 11 18 25	3 10 17 24 31	7 14 21 28	5 12 19 26	2 9 16 23 30	7 14 21 28	4 11 18 25	1 8 15 22 29	6 13 20 27	3 10 17	2 8 15 22 29	5 12 19 26	2 9 16 23	2 9 16 23 30

PREPARE (Identify)

1. Business case — approve, identify and define sustainability reporting team and its coordinator
2. Reporting team to go through guidelines and propose 'in accordance level'
3. Produce Development Plan (CPA/PERT)
4. Kick-off meeting – 'buy-in and sponsor'
5. Engage internal stakeholders (GRI Aspect Table)

CONNECT (Wide Range of Stakeholders)

6. Identify stakeholders
7. Prioritise stakeholders

(Continued)

8	**Engage stakeholders – Topics Table – record aspects – identify why and who**
9	**Build stakeholder relationships**
10	Regular progress meetings
	DEFINE (Prioritise and Validate Key Stakeholders)
11	**Determine material aspects**
12	**Determine boundary of material items**
13	**Produce materiality matrix and determine 'thresholds'**
14	**Validate material aspects**
15	Regular progress meetings
	MONITOR
16	**Decision makers approve aspects and indicators to be monitored**

(Continued)

	Task
17	Monitor material aspects and set policies and procedures to measure as necessary
18	Set SMART goals and targets
19	Regular progress meetings
	REPORT (Review)
20	Develop narrative for statement
21	Draft sustainability/ integrated report
22	Regular progress meetings
23	GRI application level check
24	Finalise the report
25	Send for publication
26	Launch report
27	Feedback

It is important that the sustainability leader does not try to do it all and that staff and other stakeholders are involved and understanding, from the outset, of the concept, that everyone is responsible for their own sustainability performance. To emphasise this point some organisations will issue all their staff with a sustainability manager card and offer formal lines of communication for training staff and collecting staff, supplier and stakeholder suggestions.

Preparing the business case – board approval

This section is not about the business case for reporting, as that has been made earlier. This is about seeking board approval, a critically important governance guidance activity from which many would benefit. The activities in red on the Critical Path Programe (CPA) in Schedule 1 show the key activities. If they are delayed or are not carried out, the programme will be delayed unless the lead sustainability coordinator and their team adjust the programme or revise the end date. The point is that CPA is an excellent way to manage the delivery of the process.

Template 1 Board Report Business Case for Sustainability Reporting

Proposal – Sustainability Reporting and Disclosure Using GRI			Item No 1

Decision Maker	Date	Title of Report	
Board	2020	Board Proposal – Sustainability Reporting and Disclosure Using GRI	
Classification for Approval		Report of Chair/CEO	
Regions Involved			
Policy Context		Corporate Narrative Reporting – Sustainability Strategy	
Financial Summary		Costs related to the processes of measurement and reporting will utilise existing staff and training budgets	
Cost Centre		Corporate Services/Sustainability	

1 Summary

Summarise how the proposal to report meets with strategic corporate objectives, values and policies. State any legislation and regulation that would be complied with. State any standards that would be complied with and any distinctions that may be obtained. State the final recommendation of the report that follows the summary.

Reporting embeds and communicates sustainable practice, through measurement, transparency and disclosure.

2 Recommendations

Recommendation to state outcome and include resources, cost and time where appropriate.

3 Previous policy/recommendations

Outline any past related approvals or failed requests as appropriate.

4 Background information

Articulate the organisation's internal and external sustainability context in relation to the Sustainability Development Goals. This should provide an overview of the sustainability reporting framework proposed as a corporate reporting instrument. This might include some details on legislation, regulation, relevant recent sector reports, peer views and those of professionals about what is considered best practice. It may also include the leadership position of the most senior decision makers. This section might also outline any anticipated successes and benefits, including changed culture implications, reduced impacts and net positive expectations.

5 Proposal

State where the organisation is as regards sustainability and environmental social governance, and where it could be and why. Discuss how it will get to where it is going. It is helpful to position the government's, stock exchanges' and regulator's position for managing sector changes and transitions if applicable in this section.

The proposal should discuss common, comparable, consistent and rankable standards and perhaps articulate an argument on the most appropriate standard considering any suitable alternatives available.

Discuss any areas of sustainability in which the organisation is already involved. Cover any size issues, supply chain issues, impact issues, integrated thinking of departments and cross-organisational thinking.

Discuss the opportunities of the reporting process, relationship building with stakeholders and the strength of influence and visibility for medium and long-term planning. Discuss the challenges and discipline and how this will be dealt with to deliver the best response, including use of interim resources, training and linking to good practice networks.

Discuss accountability, audit and governance to maximise constructive and proactive responses using systematic approaches. A sustainability report shows how an organisation manages its impacts. GRI defines the metrics for the topics to be measured, including carbon, energy, waste, water, biodiversity, emissions, contamination, remediation, diversity, health and safety, employment, investment and growth, design standards, procurement, community, corruption, R&D, product and service labelling, marketing and so on. Some organisations might want to draft the 'in accordance' option and possible relevant topics subject to the outcome of the reporting process. They might also want to speculate on the implications of sector position and leadership in maximising and articulating future opportunities.

6 *Programme of works*

Produce a programme such as Schedule 1, if possible, or a schedule like this one and state by which time the organisation could achieve GRI:

Approve – the proposal	Date. . .
Prepare – action plan, kick-off meeting	Date. . .
Connect – with stakeholders	Date. . .
Define – materiality boundary and metrics	Date. . .
Monitor – data (quality processes)	Date. . .
Communicate – prepare report	Date. . .
Report – launch	Date. . .

7 *Financial implications*

The operational costs for delivering the reporting process should be calculated, and the cost benefit from income generation and expenditure savings should be calculated. Any capital costs, resource costs, training and staffing costs should also be identified. Where possible, the finances should be scheduled over multiple years, which may include areas of qualitative response for benefits over time. A top tip for many organisations is to book key staff in a sustainability course run by experts such as Total Eco Management; the benefits should far outweigh the cost. Companies that are time poor may prefer to outsource sustainability reporting support; again, experts can guide you. Ensure publishing and audit costs are considered as applicable; however, many organisations do not have these costs. Annual costs after year one should mainly be contained within existing department budgets.

Sustainability has many 'soft' topics, but increasingly monetisation and actual measurement of income and expenditures resulting from sustainability practices enable companies to assess the impact on profit. Good examples include the EU Carbon Trading Scheme, PES Payments for Ecosystem Services and Biodiversity Offsetting with metrics £/tCO$_2$/ha/yr for planting trees and sequestration.

It is important to note that GRI is a public for good, and there is no cost to buy or download the standard, or even pay for being associated with GRI. This is important because association with many other standards must be acquired at a cost. In addition, GRI is self-certified and does not impose extra costs.

Of course, there may be specific economic, social and environmental benefits, including reduced emissions, waste, effluents, water and so on, which have an impact on the planet. Indeed, some may directly generate income from renewable energy generation (i.e. photovoltaics providing surplus energy back to the grid for a revenue return).

8 Human resource and establishment matters

Discuss staffing positions, securing buy-in and activities to encourage staff involvement.

9 Any other risks

Risk relates primarily to brand and reputation status changes, so discuss any concerns about the costs to report being considered prohibitive. The challenge is to find a process that enables and supports change so that the organisation is not left behind. Discuss failure to achieve the standards and how extra support can be found for this.

Be aware of using the wrong metrics and/or making the wrong triangulations; GRI is the standard for government departments, institutions and the market that leading organisations have used for several years.

There may be difficulties with stakeholder participation; methods to secure involvement and participation need to be carefully considered for effectiveness and cost. Effective planning and facilitation often require experienced practitioners of stakeholder engagement to mitigate the risk of poor responses and failure to secure buy-in.

There will also be pressure to improve year after year, possible exposure of major gaps in practice and data, and consideration of rare but unforeseen adverse impacts relative to how well processes are managed and governed by the organisation. Good levels of commitment and engagement, plus the right competencies, will help to mitigate the risks.

10 Environmental/sustainability matters

Discuss environmental social governance matters in the context of the organisation and its business sector. There are likely to be matters of leadership, measurement of the usual suspects (materials, waste water, energy, emissions, biodiversity, ecology, well-being and meters for the same), plus issues where, say, utilities are not metered or multi-let leasing situations where actions are needed to install equipment to secure the data, meaning partial data can be reported initially.

The task at hand should not be underestimated. Organisations will have to undergo the biggest change management programme since Victorian times.

The potential to consider and create green jobs should also not be underestimated.

11 Diversity impact

It is important to note that organisational strength can come from proper and due consideration of diversity issues. It remains the elephant in the room, including equal pay, and organisations should self-reflect on where they are and be proactive and proud to run equitable businesses.

Organisations should not be complacent on such issues but should come off the sidelines and show respect to themselves and the nations of the world, especially those that are excluded and marginalised.

12 Recommendation

The organisation will pursue the GRI standard 'in accordance' Core option by (fill in the date) with a budget of (fill in the amount). The report author and his/her team will be responsible.

It's time for action. 'In God we trust; all others must bring data'.

Checklist (Sign-off)

Department	Checked By	Date
Chair		
CEO		
Other relevant directors		

Setting out

Once the board or senior person's approval has been obtained, the organisation will have achieved a key aspect of governance which is recorded and saved in the usual way. The organisation is now ready to set out on its journey to report.

This book enables organisations to complete the journey well and be supported and guided every step of the way. The journey is flexible and enables an organisaton's own style, own needs and own context to be reflected.

The journey is represented in Diagram 3, but, in any case, the process will unfold in the chapters that follow.

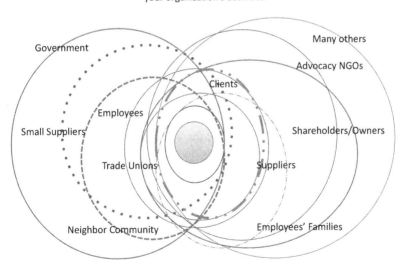

Stakeholders are individuals (or groups) who affect – or are affected by your organization's activities.

Diagram 3 GRI Sustainability Reporting Process

Prepare – This is mainly the internal part of the journey: to plan the reporting process. First get top management 'buy-in' and interdepartmental inclusion for integrated approaches following board/senior person/'s approval. Hold a kick-off meeting with relevant staff, consider corporate strategy and risks and opportunities for sustainability, identify issues, discuss time, costs and resourcing. It is important to have a kick-off meeting that begins with the end in mind.

Connect – This is mainly the 'external' part of the journey: to identify and prioritise stakeholders who have the greatest influence, both positive and negative, on the organisation and/or its impacts. It involves discussions with a broad range of stakeholders to identify the issues to address. It further targets the building of long-term relationships with stakeholders. Record how stakeholders engaged, when they engaged, topics identified and why and where they were important.

Define – This stage gathers the material from the Prepare and Connect phases, the 'goal is to choose' the most significant impacts to be managed and changed by the organisation. This involves a narrower team of stakeholders than the Connect stage for the purpose of selecting the most material areas to be reported on, to identify the boundary of reporting and to validate capability.

Monitor – This phase is about the focussed collection of quality data. Policies, protocols and procedures are adjusted to facilitate data collection through cross-functional and integrated efforts that may also be cross-organisational if the reporting boundary includes external suppliers. This phase involves data recording, monitoring and review.

Report – This involves getting the report drafted and finalised, looking at the format, production and publication. This phase looks at the dynamics to optimise engagement and feedback. And remember, celebrate the report.

When reporting, it is important to be able to articulate the process for defining the report's content and its topics and boundaries; indeed, GRI Standards specifically asks this question. The answer revolves around the organisation's response to its sustainability context across the Prepare, Connect and Define phases, so take care that good records are kept. This is a useful early hint that will make writing the report quicker and easier – 'forewarned is forearmed', as they say.

Reporting is a living cycle of continuous improvement that monitors what is material and what matters in the areas of greatest impact for the purpose of improving company performance and accountability.

The Prepare phase is crucial as it represents the opportunity for solid planning of the program, employee responsibilities, budget, timetable and target outcome (i.e. 'in accordance' Core option). It is an opportunity to galvanise resources and gain a shared commitment and agreement across the organisation and with key stakeholders that a sustainability report is to be delivered.

As we proceed through the process, you will gather the necessary approvals and records. For many companies the first stage is usually a paper to the board, setting out the business case to report. Board approval reflects the fact that sustainability is a valuable investment in the business and recommends that the company apply appropriate resources to deliver the report by an agreed time, which is an important strategic decision. The activities required to deliver the report must be planned, and, like many activities, it requires good management and use of performance evaluation review techniques to deliver the report on time, within budget and of the required quality. Once approved, an organisation can hold a kick-off meeting covering the context surrounding the organisation, its business model and goals, team and operational structures, stakeholder approach, support to achieve its targets and so on. A key issue is getting the right people to the meeting. An example of an agenda for a kick-off meeting can be found in Chapter 2, 'Prepare'.

2 Prepare

For didactic purposes the Prepare phase should take one month of the year-long process identified in Schedule 2. During this month, the focus is on the following activities:

Schedule 2 Prepare Phase Timeline

		April				
		1	8	15	22	29
PREPARE (Identify)						
1	Identify and define sustainability reporting team and its coordinator	�				
2	Reporting team to go through guidelines and propose 'in accordance' option	▓	▓			
3	Produce Development Plan (CPA/PERT)			▓		
4	Kick-off meeting – 'buy-in and sponsor'				▓	
5	Engage internal stakeholders (GRI Topic Table)					▓

Let's start with identifying and assembling the sustainability team.

Assembling the team

This is very straightforward. The lead sustainability coordinator and senior officer can call a meeting of the organisation's departmental directors (this might be the standard 'Executive Meeting'), who should agree they will each respectively identify a lead person in their department to attend a kick-off meeting.

There have been times when we have attended departmental meetings with the twofold effect of explaining sustainability reporting and the organisation's purpose but also to select motivated leaders within the departments to work towards the integrated management and achievement of the organisation's sustainability report. Those selected were asked to read the modules of the GRI Standards and/or the standards proposed to be used.

GRI does not really advise on the constituency of the sustainability team, other than that there should be cross-departmental representation. GRI's intention is that this should bring about the strategic and cultural focus needed to identify and apply changes.

Understanding the GRI Standards and choosing the 'in accordance' option

GRI has a framework comprising six modules. These contain the Requirements for Disclosure. The modules can be used individually or together. They are used through the processes detailed in Figure 4.

The modules consist of:

- 101 Foundation – This provides a great introduction to the Standards. It details the 'Reporting Principles' to be followed by organisations in the production of a sustainability report, SIMC and CRAB TC, as we learnt in the Chapter 1.
- 102 General Disclosures – These are organisational disclosures about the context, culture and processes the organisation uses.
- 103 Management Approach – These are disclosures required to report on an organisation's approach to the 'key topics' within the topic-specific modules: social, environmental and economic. The organisation explains why a topic is material, how each material topic is managed and how performance is evaluated for the setting of targets.

Topic-specific standards are detailed within modules 200, 300 and 400, respectively. These are the economic, environmental and social topics, and their topic-specific disclosures. Management approach and topic-specific disclosures work together.

Following the board's approval, and during the 'assembling the team' discussions, the lead sustainability coordinator can engage the team to develop a view on whether they want to achieve the 'in accordance Core option' or the 'In Accordance Comprehensive Option'.

This is a very important step and should not be missed. Most companies identify what it is they want to deliver as an outcome early on. This provides the team with direction, focus and a clear picture of where they are trying to get to. This is a good stage to consult the GRI Sustainability Disclosure Database: http://database.globalreporting.org/ (over 50,000 sustainability reports from organisations around the world, in all sectors and all sizes) to compare the material topics, disclosures and performance of peer organisations. The style of the reports can also be compared.

GRI recognises three types of reports, but only Core and Comprehensive options are in accordance with the GRI Standards.

1   Core indicates that the report contains the minimum information needed to understand the nature of the organisation, its material topics and related impacts and how these are managed.
2   Comprehensive builds on the Core option by requiring additional disclosures on the organisation's strategy, ethics and integrity, and governance. In addition, the organisation is required to report more extensively on its impacts by reporting all of the topic-specific disclosures for each material topic covered by the Standards.

Please note that the two options are not necessarily a measure of how good the organisation is at reporting; instead, they reflect the degree to which the standard has been applied. It is the organisation's choice whether or not to progress from Core to Comprehensive; the organisation should decide what best meets the needs of its stakeholders.

A sustainability report must contain a claim as a self-declaration on the 'in accordance' option of either Core or Comprehensive. However, the GRI Standards seek to be welcoming of organisations that are starting out, or for whatever reason are not quite at the Core option capacity to report, so GRI has the 'GRI-referenced' option (i.e. if the organisation does not reach the minimum criteria for Core, it cannot make the claim that its report has been prepared in accordance with the GRI Standards). In these cases, a GRI-referenced option is required to be included in any published materials identifying the specific social, economic and environmental disclosures, including the management approach which has been used.

To be clear the two options, Core and Comprehensive, are 'in accordance' options. The GRI-referenced option is available to companies reporting to a lesser extent than Core option.

Generally speaking, GRI recommends that first-time reporters aim to produce a report prepared 'in accordance with the GRI Standard: Core option'. I have written this very specifically, as this is how GRI requires a 'claim' of 'in accordance' to appear in the sustainability report.

The main differences between a Core report and a Comprehensive report is that the latter requires greater detail and a greater number of disclosures, as shown in Table 2.1.

The 'in accordance Core option' requires 33 Standard Disclosures to be responded to. The 'in accordance Comprehensive option' requires all 56 Standard Disclosures to be responded to.

Whether a report is Core or Comprehensive, there is a total of 85 specific Standard Disclosures from which to choose.

At various points in the Prepare, Connect and especially the Define phases, the question as to how topics are defined, calculated (qualitative and quantitative metrics, denominators and numerators), documented and so on will need clarification as to what is meant. Various stakeholders can pop up at any time and ask for an example of how emissions under Environmental 305 are calculated, and how they should be compiled and reported. This is when the GRI Standards Environmental Module comes into its own and the lead sustainability coordinator needs to be on hand to access the guidance for the disclosure, either online or turning to the correct pages of a hard copy of the relevant module, which should be used as a key reference to ensure that any data provided meets the GRI criteria.

A reporter also has the option to use the Sector Disclosures if they want to be more attuned to the topics of their sector. Sector Disclosures are sets of disclosures specifically designed for a sector of work, developed from

Table 2.1. GRI In Accordance Option Disclosures

REQUIRED DISCLOSURES		
Disclosures	*'In accordance' – Core*	*'In accordance' – Comprehensive*
101 Foundation	Applying the 10 Reporting Principles for Content and Quality	Applying the 10 Reporting Principles for Content and Quality
102 Standard Disclosures	33 Disclosures	56 Disclosures
103 Management Approach	Report on all material topics	Report on all material topics
Topic-Specific Disclosures	There are 33 topics, 85 Disclosures	There are 33 topics, 85 Disclosures
200 Economic **300** Environmental **400** Social	At least one Disclosure related to each identified material topic	All Disclosures related to each identified material topic
Disclosures from Sectors Disclosures	Optional, if available for the organisation's sector	Optional, if available for the organisation's sector

the main GRI guidelines, in the format of the main guidelines and as a fine-tuned version for a sector. However, they are straightforward to use; the organisation checks whether or not a sector disclosure is applicable and responds to all of the specific Standard Disclosures, topic-specific disclosures and requirements of the management approach for the sector.

Sector Disclosures are available in electronic GRI Standards format to download free from GRI's website: www.globalreporting.org. The number of Sector Disclosures continues to increase; the present ten include:

Airport Operators
Construction and Real Estate
Electric Utilities
Event Organisers
Financial Services
Food Processing
Media
Mining and Metals
NGO (Non-Governmental Organisation)
Oil and Gas

Development Plan

Once the 'in accordance' option has been chosen, the lead sustainability coordinator can develop a project-specific timeline deploying the organisation's appropriate resources across the various actions in the program.

It is critical that reporting the Development Plan allows adequate time to reflect on and define the material topics to be reported on and where their impacts should be managed and changed.

Experience shows that many organisations underestimate the time needed for this. Many companies tell us if they had performed the prepare phase better, they would have avoided many problems that affected the content and quality of their final report.

Using the critical path Performance Evaluation Techniques, the Development Plan is a key feature to track the management of the process. It is likely there will be revisions of the Development Plan and possibly even to the personnel involved. It will also require engagement of the board and the regular engagement of executive team members. For these reasons, it is important to have a regular meeting agenda set for the entire reporting cycle until the launch of the report, as detailed in Schedule 1.

Kick-off meeting (agreement on the reporting process) and engaging internal stakeholders

The kick-off meeting is a formal meeting chaired by the CEO or equivalent; it is also not unusual for it to be chaired by the lead sustainability coordinator supported by a GRI expert.

Invitations to attend will often have gone to key board members (sponsors), the cross-departmental sustainability team members and key management employees important to delivering policy and procedures. Many organisations might invite a small number of key first-tier suppliers subject to their level of influence on the products or services provided.

The purpose of the meeting is to encourage connectivity and secure 'buy-in', to engage, to secure understanding and begin wider involvement. As the Chinese say,

> *Tell me and I will forget,*
> *Show me and I may remember,*
> *Involve me and I will understand.*

The meeting helps to gather reporting momentum, it galvanises a wider reporting team, it states the organisation's sustainability reporting objectives and current and proposed sustainability activity, and, most importantly, begins stakeholder dialogue by asking and discussing what topics they consider most important to the organisation to monitor and report on. The meeting participants are given the GRI Standards Topics Table (see Table 2.2) with its three categories (environmental, social and economic) and 33 topics; the participants are asked to each identify the five topics they consider most important for impacting the organisation's day-to-day corporate activity.

In summary, the Topics Table reveals that the GRI Standards are made up of the three categories: economic, environmental and social. The categories generate 33 topics. And there are 85 disclosures (in parentheses) associated with the topics.

The Topics Table will appear again in the connect phase when engaging with external stakeholders, but for now, record and gather the results and end the meeting by stating the actions arising and setting times for their completion and by whom.

Many organisations are unsure what to place on the agenda of a kick-off meeting, so we have set out the type of best practice example we use at Total Eco Management on a helpful indicative agenda shown next.

Table 2.2 Categories and Topics in the GRI Standards

Category	Economic	Environmental
Topics III	Economic Performance (4) Market Presence (2) Indirect Economic Impacts (2) Procurement Practices (1) Anti-Corruption (3) Anti-Competitive Behaviour (1)	Materials (3) Energy (5) Water and Effluents (5 effective from January 2021) Biodiversity (4) Emissions (7) Effluents and Waste (5) Environmental Compliance (1) Supplier Environmental Assessment (2)

Social

Sub-Categories	Labour Practices and Decent Work	Human Rights	Society	Product Responsibility
Topics III	Employment (3) Labour/Management Relations (1) Occupational Health and Safety (10 effective from January 2021) Training and Education (3) Diversity and Equal Opportunity (2)	Non-discrimination (1) Freedom of Association and Collective Bargaining (1) Child Labour (1) Forced or Compulsory Labour (1) Security Practices (1) Rights of Indigenous People (1) Human Rights Assessment (3)	Local Communities (2) Supplier Social Assessment (2) Public Policy (1)	Customer Health and Safety (2) Marketing and Labelling (3) Customer Privacy (1) Socio-economic Compliance (1)

Template 2 Kick-off Meeting Agenda

**KICK-OFF MEETING (SEEKING AGREEMENT ON
THE REPORTING PROCESS) AGENDA**

Attendees: Chair, Relevant Board (Sponsor), CEO, CFO, Sustainability
Coordinator, Green Champions, Data Champions, Interested Staff, Lead
Sustainability Coordinator

Introduction

> Refer to the approved business case; what is sought to be achieved
> Discussion on what the report will contain and how to prepare it
> Sustainability context and Sustainable Development Goals
> Why sustainability is important
> Introduction to the GRI Standards (invited speaker)
> Material business topics and impacts – interactive exercise –
> environmental, economic, social (Table 2.2). Participants to select five.

Strategic business goals
Timeline to report
Budget – action plan, training, launch
The team and operational structure
Stakeholders – what approach and support
Initial view of final report – audience and review
Sustainability messaging to the public – signage
Actions agreed upon
Any other business
Next meeting

3 Connect (wide range of stakeholders)

From the solid bedrock that is the Sustainability Context to the firm foundations of Prepare the organisation is ready to build a robust structure that needs to be made watertight through stakeholder engagement to enable the organisation to provide accountability to its stakeholders. The KPMG's International Survey of Corporate Sustainability Reporting 2017 says that many organisations fail to engage stakeholders well.

Schedule 3 is an extract from Schedule 1, which shows the reporting process across the five-stage journey. As can be seen from Schedule 3, the Connect phase of the journey focuses on broad engagement with a wide range of stakeholders. We will see how straightforward it is to identify which stakeholders have the greatest influence. We will then show you a best practice method to prioritise those stakeholders who can add the most value when engaged with. Once we know which stakeholders are best to focus

Schedule 3 Connect Phase Timeline

		April					May			
		1	8	15	22	29	5	12	19	26
	CONNECT (Wide Range of Stakeholders)									
6	Identify stakeholders									
7	Prioritise stakeholders									
8	Engage stakeholders – Topics Table – record topics, identify why and who									
9	Build stakeholder relationships									
10	Regular progress meetings									

our efforts on, we will show you how to enter into dialogue and enhance this relationship to make it a more useful long-term one.

For years we have argued that organisations cannot properly report unless they can incorporate the most significant external impacts arising as a result of their products and services, including operational impacts (where product and service efficiencies can have bad life cycle impacts). Some good examples to think about here are retailers, electronic equipment manufacturers and supermarkets that have environmental and social footprints ten times larger than the operations they own and control. (It identifies the extent to which the organisation 'contributes' to the impact caused by a topic from its own activities or those resulting from its direct relationships.) GRI Standards brings together the discussion on relevant topics and impacts with the supply chain and customers with their contribution to impact. This is a powerful way to understand and encourage cross-organisational learning that serves to reinforce the integrated thinking promoted by following the processes in this book.

Identify stakeholders

An organisation might have thousands of different stakeholders. Engaging with key stakeholders is an integral part of the reporting process.

Depending on the size of the company, this can typically be done in under an hour with the right personnel in one room (or on a Webex-type call). The lead sustainability coordinator, the CEO and the finance director or their equivalent make a great core team. The objective is to ensure that we have the gatekeepers who decide and sign off on who is and who is not impacted by the organisation. Sales, procurement and buying directors are also similarly useful depending on the type of organisation.

The following are some of the factors that an organisation should initially consider when selecting key stakeholders:

- *Responsibility:* those linked to an organisation through legal, financial, operational regulations, contracts and/or policies.
- *Influence:* those who have the ability to influence whether or not an organisation can reach its intended goals. This can include those with informal influence or those with formal decision-making power, internally or externally.
- *Dependency:* those who are most dependent on your organisation, customers/clients reliant on your products or services, or suppliers for which you are a large client.
- *Proximity:* those who the organisation depends on for daily operations and those living close to your operating sites.

- *Representation:* those who represent key institutions with whom your organisation interacts, such as trade union representatives, community leaders, local politicians and so on.

It is important to remark that there are also stakeholders who are indirectly influenced by the organisation's operations but may play an important role when assessing risks and opportunities, such as experts (i.e. consultants or other sustainability specialists who provide support to organisations) to select stakeholders, engage stakeholders, identify and determine what is material and where, write reports and so on.

The lead sustainability coordinator simply makes a list of all the organisations and stakeholders, sorted by sector, who affect or are affected by the organisation and its activities. You can show the simple example of stakeholders in Diagram 4 to help them in identifying a full list of organisations, and individuals where relevant, applicable to your organisation.

Use Table 3.1 to list stakeholders under each of the headings.

Prioritise stakeholders

The selection of stakeholders and how to engage them has a direct impact on the selection of material issues.

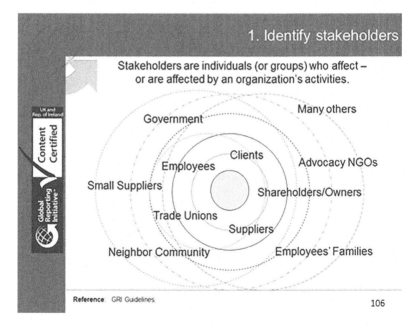

Diagram 4 Stakeholders That Affect an Organisation – Identification

Many organisations want to know where best to focus their limited resources when liaising with stakeholders. They also want a simple and objective prioritisation methodology. The following shows you how easy this is to achieve, as we use it regularly in both corporate sustainability training and working with organisations as consultants on stakeholder engagement.

After identifying the stakeholders, we must prioritise them, and a great tool which we use to do this is the Stakeholder Prioritisation Table (Table 3.1). The organisation simply lists their actual stakeholders in the left-hand-side stakeholder column. Each stakeholder is then scored '1' in the corresponding box for every 'Yes' answer, and a zero for every 'No' answer. The scores are totalled, and those evaluated as having a higher score have the greatest connection to the organisation and are the highest priority for engagement during the reporting process.

The outcome at this stage is thus a prioritised list of stakeholders from which the organisation can decide whom to engage on an informed basis. These stakeholders selected can be worked with on the reporting journey, developing collective understanding of the issues and managing change for your organisation. It is easy to appeciate that the incorporation of key suppliers can be very powerful to improving the quality of the reporting organisation's products and services but also to securing more complete data on material topics.

Frameworks like GRI are shining a spotlight on supply chains. It is recognised that gathering data from within only the reporting organisation often represents the tip of the iceberg. It is the supply chain that represents the main bulk and the main impact, so we must look deeper to understand the impacts better.

Stakeholder engagement

The way organisations engage with stakeholders and the questions they ask of them will help to identify material topics.

Connect phase engagement generally deploys a wider range of methods; these are predominantly for external organisations, as can be seen in Diagram 5, showing stakeholder groups engaged, the mediums used to engage and how often the engagements happen through questionnaires, email, intranet, Webex, social media, meetings with stakeholders, NGOs, governments and others, membership in sector task groups, constant dialogue, stakeholder events, visitor centers, mystery shoppers, interviews, telephone, letters, posters, blogs, newsletters, feedback on reports and policies, and so on. In larger organisations, there will also be a need to engage with employees (including subsidiaries), who can benefit from the same consultation methods.

Having identified and prioritised stakeholders, the next task is to action the engagement. One of the most effective ways of doing this is to ask stakeholders – using the various media options – which five topics of the

Table 3.1 Stakeholder Prioritisation

Total €co Management Ltd.
Sustainability Consulting & Reporting, GRI Certified Training

Prioritise stakeholders

A schedule of stakeholders that can be prioritised to determine who best to consult - 'Influence on stakeholder assessments and decisions' and 'Significance of the organization's economic, environmental and social impacts'

Yes = 1
No = 0

Stakeholders (Consultation method)	Does this group stongly influence your			Is this group strongly influenced by your			Will this group strongly influence or be strongly influenced in the future?	Total
	Econ Performance	Social Performance	Env Performance	Econ Performance	Social Performance	Env Performance		
Employees (surveys, emails, train, procedures)	1	1	0	1	1	1	1	6
Customers								
Suppliers (mtgs, train, induction, audit)								
Local Community (public mtgs, media, procedures)								
Clients (mtgs, events, email, soc media)								
Investors (corp reports, AGM, mtgs)								
Regulators								
Statutory Authorities								
Competitors (multi stakeholder initiatives)								
NGO's								

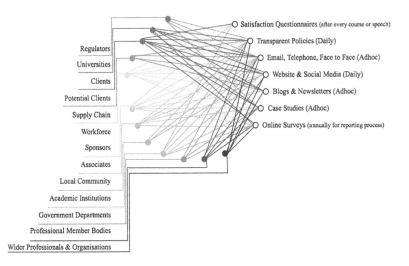

Diagram 5 Stakeholder Groups Engaged, How Consulted, and How Often

organisation's day-to-day activities they consider most important for the organisation to monitor and report on.

The following provides an excellent template for straightforward consultation. Any organisation, large or small, can simply copy the template, brand it and use it to gather the views of their stakeholders. The template,, along with many others, was downloadable as part of some GRI-certified software that Total Eco Management developed for GRI for G4; similar software that produces a complete GRI Standards Sustainability Report and the associated documents will hopefully be developed soon. Intelligent software, such as SRT, helps companies through the process and to the final product (the sustainability report, GRI Gold Standard compliant or not), but nevertheless a report to enable companies to show that sustainability matters to them and operational processes are in place for better business performance, which is a key issue for investors.

Template 3 Stakeholder Engagement

Connect – Stakeholder Engagement (Insert your company logo in the template title)

(Insert company name) is serious about sustainability and is committed to working with our stakeholders to improve our business value and be a positive influence serving society.

(Insert company name – outline your organisation's business model and supply chain values)

As part of our GRI/organisational stakeholder engagement process, we are asking key stakeholders which topics you consider most important for our company to monitor and report on for the achievement of global sustainable development (refer to the Sustainability Categories and Topics Sheet below and attached).

We are aware of our stakeholders' influence on the products/services we provide. We want to develop knowledge that will enable us to prioritise issues you consider to be material to (Insert company name).

Please follow the following methodology.

Identify five material areas from the attached Sustainability Categories and Topics Sheet which you consider to be issues that should be material to (Insert company name).

Feel free to comment on how you came to your selected outcome for each topic (i.e. Emissions, because it supports the delivery of a Sustainable Development Goal; 13 Climate Change; and 12 Responsible Consumption) by seeking accurate carbon footprint data, reduced fuel use and reduced corporate expenditures going forward.

Tick the final box if you are happy for us to call and discuss any responses.

Topic 1:
Comment   . . . .
. . . .
. . . .

Topic 2:
Comment   . . . .
. . . .
. . . .

Topic 3:
Comment   . . . .
. . . .
. . . .

Topic 4:
Comment   . . . .
. . . .
. . . .

Topic 5:
Comment   . . . .
. . . .
. . . .

Any general comments or further topics: _____

_____

_____

_____

_____

_____

_____

_____

_____

Company/Organisation_____

Print Name _____

_____

Position_____

I would be grateful for your response by return, or at your earliest conveni-ence to (Insert an email contact and telephone contact number).

Please tick this box if you are happy for us to give you a call: ☐

The lead sustainability coordinator prioritises each response from the topics list, beginning with the topics with the most to those with the least. The resulting list is carried over into the Define stage.

Sustainability Categories and Topics Sheet

Category	Economic	Environmental
Topics III	Economic Performance (4) Market Presence (2) Indirect Economic Impacts (2) Procurement Practices (1) Anti-Corruption (3) Anti-Competitive Behaviour (1)	Materials (3) Energy (5) Water (3) Biodiversity (4) Emissions (7) Effluents and Waste (5) Environmental Compliance (1) Supplier Environmental Assessment (2)

Social

Sub-Categories	Labour Practices and Decent Work	Human Rights	Society	Product Responsibility
Topics III	Employment (3) Labour/Management Relations (1) Occupational Health and Safety (4) Training and Education (3) Diversity and Equal Opportunity (2)	Non-discrimination (1) Freedom of Association and Collective Bargaining (1) Child Labour (1) Forced or Compulsory Labour (1) Security Practices (1) Rights of Indigenous People (1) Human Rights Assessment (3)	Local Communities (2) Supplier Social Assessment (2) Public Policy (1)	Customer Health and Safety (2) Marketing and Labelling (3) Customer Privacy (1) Socio-economic Compliance (1)

Build stakeholder relationships

A major part of the Connect phase is the opportunity to build relationships. A common method of engagement is to invite key stakeholders to an initial meeting that includes workshops and facilitators. The participants are encouraged to contribute ideas, practices and their own sustainability data as it applies to material topics and so on, all assistance that they believe would improve products, services, relationships, save money, generate efficiencies, contribute to Sustainable Development Goals and so on. Sustainability is the key theme; groups are asked to discuss sustainability topics and suggest priorities and why. Thereafter, feedback from each group should be summarised and recorded to be part of the conversation when prioritising the material topics. To get the constructive juices flowing, we would include appropriate team-building exercises and encourage cross-organisational dialogue and networking. Encourage the search and use of the best practices they have seen and are hearing about across the sector.

These types of meetings can be just the beginning of some great ongoing relationships. A common response of participants of these workshops is 'wow'. It has produced a far wider field of vision and ideas to improve income and reduce costs whilst reducing impacts; great knowledge on where impacts of the business lie; and the areas that partners prioritise as important and will work with them to change. Many a director emerging from this stakeholder engagement comments that that they would like to implement the same at their own organisations, having learned a lot that is relevant and knowing there is a mechanism for being listened to regarding innovative contributions.

Even if Template 3 for stakeholder consultation is used as is, it is designed to encourage long-term relationships. These have the following benefits for the reporting organisation:

> Provides different perspectives on an organisation's strengths and weaknesses
> Helps to avoid unexpected criticisms
> Helps to proactively identify problems
> Increases acceptance of topics chosen as material
> Builds a positive external impression of an organisation
> Provides knowledge on specific sustainability topics

Although in our experience these benefits are more immediately visible in a facilitated meeting with a workshop format, we find it important for organisations to use an array of minimal-cost platforms to interact with stakeholders.

4   Define

The Define phase is about the 'prioritisation' of material topics and how the organisation has contributed to causing the impact either directly or indirectly; the boundary for an organisation's activities; and validation of the material topics to be reported upon.

It should be remembered that 'not all topics are created equal'; in some cases, the material issue may not be relevant to the internal operations of a company, whereas in others it may be relevant in the extended supply chain; i.e. child labour may not be a problem in the UK for a clothes factory owner (direct contribution to the topic impact) but might be a problem in outsourced factories (indirect contribution by the supply chain contract to the topic impact), say, in Bangladesh. Boundary is about the reporting organisation's contribution as a result of its business activities and identifying who and where in the supply chain it occurs.

Boundaries and supply chains are important because they are an effort to provide a complete footprint of an impact and its causes and contributions.

Schedule 4 Define Phase Timeline

		June				
		3	10	17	24	31
DEFINE (Prioritise and Validate – Key Stakeholders)						
11	Determine material topics					
12	Determine boundary of material topics					
13	Produce materiality matrix and determine 'thresholds'					
14	Validate material topics					
15	Regular progress meetings					

Failure to do this for the areas measured, known as the 'material topics', results in an inaccurate assessment of impact. The GRI Standards acknowledge this limitation in each organisation's calculation of topic impact. This is significant as organisations will need time and often adjusted agreements, procedures and protocols to ensure the collection of data from supply chain members. In GRI's requirements to report and explain, they allow reporting organisations longer periods of time to collect unavailable information from supply chain members. The drive is that in the mid-term, reporters will be able to provide complete information on material impacts (i.e. the full extent of the reporting organisation's contributions).

GRI Standards acknowledge that data collection is a journey and, over time, organisations are expected to develop processes for boundary setting to gain further understanding of indirect impacts. Indeed, these expectations are based on the UN Guiding Principles on Business and Human Rights and the Organisation for Economic Cooperation and Development Guidelines on Multinational Enterprises.

Diagram 6 provides an overview for defining report content and boundary. The importance of identifying and prioritising what is material is central to reporting, yet few reporters do this in each report cycle, according to the KPMG's International Survey of Corporate Sustainability Reporting 2017. The same survey found that 41% of organisations

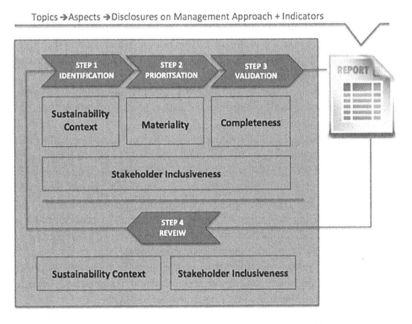

Diagram 6 Overview of Process for Defining Report Content and Boundary

could not even explain the process of defining what is material. Well, now you can.

It is important to note stakeholders, including future generations, who should be recognised by proxies (i.e. response to the Sterne Review to create a sustainable planet for future generations). GRI recognises that organisations can self-identify topics beyond the Sustainability Categories and Topic Sheet presented in Template 3.

Now you may have already picked up from reading this book that the amount of stakeholders involved differs depending on the stages of the reporting process. The stages of the process are as follows:

1   The first stage of *Identification* involves a broad range of relevant topics and engagement with a broad range of stakeholders.
2   The second stage of *Prioritisation* involves a smaller range of stakeholders, mainly internal, though some external.
3   The third stage of *Validation* has an even smaller group of stakeholders (i.e. executive team company owners).
4   The fourth stage of *Review* returns to a broad range of relevant topics and stakeholders as with identification in stage 1.

Determine the material topics

GRI Standards focus on significant impacts that are caused or contributed to by the organisation or that are linked to its activities' products or services by its relationship with its suppliers. GRI is not only interested in the direct causal link, but it goes beyond that as to whether or not an organisation has contributed to an impact via its supply chain.

Defining what is material, and where it matters, is arguably the main focal point of sustainability reporting, as such it is important that organisations know how to do this.

It should be noted that the outcome of this 'determine the material topics' phase will impact the journey considerably. We should be aware at the outset that the objective is to identify what matters most. It's like packing a backpack for a hike – you bring only the supplies that are absolutely critical, otherwise the weight will slow you down and eventually bring you to your knees.

Essentially, at the beginning of the Define phase, an organisation has a long list of material topics from having cast a wide net with a broad range of stakeholders and capturing their views and support.

In Define we reduce the number of stakeholders to those few who are the most knowledgeable, experienced and hold the most corporate strategic authority. We liken this transition to panning for gold.

The sieving process involves the selected stakeholders, the lead sustainability coordinator and perhaps key members of this team using a methodology called materiality testing.

A helpful example of this is the London Olympic Games. LOCOG (the London Organising Committee for the Olympic Games) prepared, planned and staged the greatest show on earth, which employed over 100,000 people at its height. The games had a huge array of national and international stakeholders; there were 12 groups of them, such as athletes and team officials, broadcasters, the general public, marketing partners, spectators, technical officials, suppliers, delivery partners, the workforce and so on, as detailed in the LOCOG 2012 Sustainability Report 'Delivering Change'. Total Eco Management was the official sustainability reporting consultant to the Olympic Games.

The types/groups of stakeholders with which LOCOG consulted for the prioritisation to determine what was material were the executives, the Olympic Games' ambassadors (an advisory group of sustainability experts) and key delivery partners (i.e. Olympic Delivery Authority and IOC) incorporating future Games. This is far fewer than the massive list of stakeholders involved in the identification phase discussed earlier. LOCOG engaged these key stakeholders around a short list of sustainability issues through several workshops and conducted an internal review, the outcome of which was the set of material issues.

A key part of the dialogue around 'boundary' relates to the supply chain (i.e. the sequence of activities and parties that provide products or services to an organisation). There are two areas to note: the first is to describe the main elements of the supply chain, explaining its characteristics and how it is composed and structured; this might be set out as a whole or in subsets. The level of detail (i.e. tier 1, tier 2, tier 3 and so on) depends on the organisation. The following example is perhaps one of the more complex relating to conflict minerals as impacts. Philips states that they do not buy minerals from the mine; they report that there are seven or more links in the supply chain between the mine and the end product, including mines to traders, exporters, smelters, refiners, alloy producers, component manufacturers and electronic equipment manufacturers. The legitimacy of the minerals is traced through 'bagging and tagging programmes' to authenticate the chain of custody. This is done using the Conflict Free Mineral Template for each supplier.

The second area you should note concerns significant changes during the reporting period (i.e. deciding to restructure the supply chain, for example, moving to another geographical location) by internalising the activity, outsourcing or discontinuing relationships with significant or strategic suppliers.

An organisation with thousands of suppliers in many countries need not worry that their challenge is greater because, with the GRI Standards, all organisations are to respond in the same narrative way as a description of their supply chain in the general disclosures. However, on a topic-specific disclosure level, more suppliers mean more organisations from whom to collect performance impact data; as such, there is increased probability that not all data is able to be obtained. However, the narrative in the management approach can describe how the organisation intends to collect full information by changing practices, contractual terms and so on over time. GRI recognises that it may take several reporting periods to achieve full disclosure of the impacts.

Produce materiality matrix and determine 'thresholds'

The outcome of the stakeholder engagement is a list of material topics. The topics must be prioritised and plotted on a 'materiality' scatter matrix. A materiality matrix shows the position of prioritised sustainability topics, the most material items being found in the upper-right-hand corner of the materiality matrix.

For each material topic the reporting organisation makes an assessment under two dimensions:

* Significance of an organisation's outward economic, environmental and social impacts
* Substantive influence on the assessments and decisions of stakeholders based on inputs from stakeholder engagement

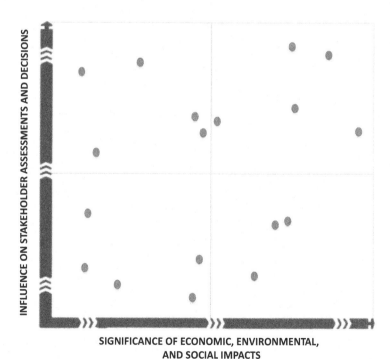

Diagram 7 Materiality Scatter Matrix

The scatter diagram should be placed in the final sustainability report.

It is important to note that a topic can be considered material based on only one dimension. At this stage a 'threshold' must be agreed upon by the key members of the sustainability coordinating team. The threshold identifies which relevant topics are sufficiently important so that it is essential to report on them. For example, the threshold could be the top four in the top right-hand quadrant of the 18 topics identified on the matrix. Or it could be six of the 18. The organisation needs to be clear on where they draw the threshold and explain why so that it is transparent how the essential topics were selected.

Once the material items are identified and prioritised, two rules apply, according to the level of reporting: a Comprehensive report requires all disclosures within the topics to be reported on. If the report is Core, the reporter must choose at least one disclosure related to each identified material topic.

Validate material topics

After the materiality test, carry out a validation to determine the availability of data. There are three questions to ask as an extension of the materiality test:

1   Is it feasible to collect the necessary information to report on the material topic in the current report period?
2   Is preparation needed to gather information on the material topics?
3   What do you need to do to gather the information?

This clarifies whether the organisation is ready to report.

After the validation, the lead sustainability coordinator writes a report to the highest governing body recommending the list of topics to be reported, and seeks approval. To avoid weaknesses in strategy and processes we recommend reconciling strategic objectives from the kick-off meeting to retain the golden thread of impacts on current and future goals. The report can respond to the following questions:

* What are the organisation's goals and main activities for the next one to two years (e.g. grow by 20%, expand operations to other cities, maintain current performance, and so on)?
* What environmental, social and economic impacts (positive and negative) does the organisation expect to cause in pursuing these goals?
* What resources are the organisation dependent on (e.g. natural resources, human resources, and so on)? What would be the result if there were a gap in any of them?

- What are the risks and opportunities that can be identified with the organisation's challenges?
- What is the organisation already doing to address these challenges? What are your peers/competitors doing to address these challenges?

Once the organisation has identified potential report content, it should then assess the adequacy of the systems for capturing and monitoring such information and disclose such on the management approach.

Disclosures on the management approach are simply a narrative description of how the organisation manages its material topics. A response is required for each topic selected, covering in the first instance why the topic was selected, how the topics and impacts are managed, and finally, how the topic is evaluated and goals set.

The management approach is important because it represents half of a disclosure on any of the 33 material topics listed in Template 3's Sustainability Categories and Topics Sheet. The management approach is about connecting the reader to the right information and explaining how the organisation identifies, analyses, manages and responds to its actual and potential impacts. The policies protocol, procedures and agreements used to manage and evaluate the topic should be identified, and the evaluation should be part of the discussion to set topic performance targets and goals.

Please also note that there is a sector-specific management approach if your sector has a Sector Disclosure. Check this against its topics and report accordingly.

Materiality is about identifying what is essential and focussing on the highest impacts, risks and matters relevant to stakeholders. If done well, the organisation will have prepared itself for the next phase (Monitor) and heeded the warning to take forward only what is needed for improving the organisation. Bringing organisations to their knees with measurement misses the point, so don't do it and aim for seamless transitions.

As we enter the data collection phase, we should be satisfied that inclusive and objective strategies have been deployed to determine the material topics and their boundary.

5 Monitor

Many would say that the hard work has now been done and approved. Setting procedures and targets, collecting data and monitoring are activities companies do all the time. Companies have well-embedded habits and find this phase the easiest to accomodate and understand. In the 21st century, good reporting, systematic collecting and monitoring of both the organisation's data and suppy chain data are necessary to acertain the bigger picture of the organisation's impacts and efficiencies.

Schedule 5 shows the key actions during the Monitor phase, but note the long duration to set policies, procedures and measures. This reflects the reality that policies and so on should develop, evolve and become fine-tuned over time.

A great benefit of the GRI Standards relative to the G3/3.1 is that less sustainability information needs to be collected. It is true that a GRI Standards report will be a disciplined and concise strategic report focussed on 'what is material and where'. However, GRI is not advising organisations to stop monitoring a diversity of sustainability-related issues; on the contrary, organisations must decide what has to be monitored in order to be managed. But a GRI Standards-based report has to be focussed on what matters and where it has to be managed and changed, resulting in a shorter report and more relevant supporting information from topics that did not get over the threshold of high priority materiality.

The main characteristic of the Monitor phase revolves around the positioning of robust procedures and checking that they are properly used for the establishment of quality monitoring information. The acronym we call 'CRAB TC', mentioned in Chapter 1, forms a set of quasi accounting principles that help organisations maintain a focus on collecting robust information. The CRAB TC principles are as follows:

Clarity means readers should be able to understand the report and its contents.

Reliability means the information can be laid out so that it can be checked.

Schedule 5 Monitor Phase Timeline

	July				August					September				October					November				December					January				February			
	31	7	14	21	28	4	11	18	25	3	10	17	24	31	7	14	21	28	5	12	19	26	2	9	16	23	30	7	14	21	28	4	11	18	25
MONITOR																																			
16 Decision makers approve topics and topics to be monitored	▓	▓																																	
17 Monitor material topics and set policies and procedures to measure as necessary					▓	▓	▓	▓	▓	▓	▓	▓	▓	▓	▓	▓	▓	▓	▓	▓	▓	▓	▓	▓	▓	▓	▓	▓	▓	▓	▓	▓			
18 Set SMART goals and targets																			▓	▓	▓	▓	▓	▓	▓	▓	▓	▓	▓	▓	▓	▓			
19 Regular progress meetings			▓			▓				▓				▓																					

Accuracy means data should be accurate and capable of being checked and reproduction used to achieve similar results.

Balance means the report should be an unbiased picture of the organisation's performance.

Timeliness means publishing on a consistent schedule.

Comparability means information is compared to past performance years and, if possible, to other organisations.

Monitor topics and set policies and procedures to measure as necessary

A report represents the organisation's sustainability performance over a fixed period, which tends to be one year, but it can be shorter or longer depending on the organisation. The goal of the Monitor phase should be to collect the required data occurring within the report period.

The monitoring of topics and the data from the disclosures are often sold as a complex business by reporting software companies, and this may feel right to large and multinational enterprises. However, the fundamentals behind monitoring are quite basic, and we see it as an altogether much simpler matter. Essentially, a table, such as Table 5.1, is all many organisations need. Some companies layer the table, building up results for the different parts of the company to reflect regions, subsidiaries and so on. Table 5.1 is effective for those wanting to keep things simple. The lead sustainability coordinator (LSC in Table 5.1) and the Sustainability Team are allocated the responsibility to regularly collect the data over the reporting period. The metric is identified as the sustainability guidance the organisation is using. Table 5.1 uses GRI metrics to track progress on a traffic light system. If the information is received in good time, it is coded Green and all is well. If it is coded Amber, the information is in delay; and if coded Red, there is a problem that needs to be addressed.

The Monitor phase identifies from whom information would most likely be obtained, when such information would likely be available or by when it would be needed. It is also important to consider ways to enhance the accuracy and reliability of the information to be reported, including identification of appropriate review processes.

The success of the Monitor phase is largely dependent on the people the organisation employs and their commitment to sustainability. We believe the key to excellence in reporting is largely about the people, so great effort is placed in finding the best people for collecting the sustainability data. (The technical side of understanding the 'business model', key capitals, and

Table 5.1 Data Collection and Monitoring

Keep track of the necessary steps in the process, including checkpoints.

Disclosure	April	May	June	July
Energy consumption within the organisation (302–1) GJ (Joules)	GJ			
Responsible for input	Energy Mgr	Energy Mgr	Energy Mgr	Energy Mgr
Check	LSC	LSC	LSC	LSC
Status				
Notes				
Energy consumption outside the organisation (302–2) GJ	GJ			
Responsible for input	Energy Mgr	Energy Mgr	Energy Mgr	Energy Mgr
Check	LSC	LSC	LSC	LSC
Status				
Notes			Overdue	Overdue
GHG emissions Scope 1 (305–1) KgCO$_2$	KgCO$_2$			
Responsible for input	Energy Mgr	Energy Mgr	Energy Mgr	Energy Mgr
Check	LSC	LSC	LSC	LSC
Status				
Notes		Overdue	Urgent	Urgent
GHG emissions Scope 2 (305–2) KgCO$_2$	KgCO$_2$			
Responsible for input	Energy Mgr	Energy Mgr	Energy Mgr	Energy Mgr
Check	LSC	LSC	LSC	LSC
Status				
Notes				

the impact of creating and sustaining value are useful when showing others how to systematically go through the reporting process.)

Set SMART goals and targets

Firms that set tangible, public sustainability goals improve their financial and environmental performance. When goals are set, a company will typically work hard to meet them and are four to five times more likely to improve their performance compared with those who do not set goals. Indeed, firms with five to ten goals show the best performance improvement, supporting the current paradigm of GRI: report only what is material.

GRI recommends that organisations establish targets for their material topics and related management approach and topics. KPMG's International Survey of Corporate Sustainability Reporting 2017 expresses concern that 13% of reports have no targets for material issues.

Defining targets can be a lengthy process for an organisation. Targets are public commitments that normally have to be embraced by the organisation as a whole; they send a positive message to shareholders and investors.

The first step is to be aware of the current performance related to each material topic and related management approach and topics. Second, it is important to know what could be improved internally and what is considered the best practice outside of the organisation. The organisation can then evaluate how much time and resources should be invested to achieve realistic targets.

Remember, targets should be SMART (Specific, Measurable, Achievable, Relevant, Time-bound) and derived from a process of listening to internal and external stakeholders.

The examples in Table 5.2 give some typical, simple targets that can be set: cutting energy use and greenhouse gas emissions and reducing water consumption and waste, all of which result in cost savings and boost the bottom line and which can result in increased employee satisfaction and productivity:

In the most sophisticated organisations, a goal leader supported by multidisciplinary teams manages each corporate sustainability goal. An increasing number of companies tie executive remuneration to sustainability goals.

Similar to the Define phase, it is good if internal and select external stakeholders are involved in setting targets.

A final point of philosophical integrity: when the bigger picture involves capacity-building and knowledge-sharing, especially between OECD- and non-OECD-based organisations, delivery of targets can be central to building a lasting legacy and organisational profile.

Table 5.2 SMART Targets

Topic/Disclosure	Target	Where Material	Why	Is Target SMART?	Goal Leader
302–4 Reduction of energy consumption GJ	+2% on 2006/07 baseline	Within and outside	Climate change, society and savings	Yes	Position
303–1 Water withdrawal by source m³/yr	11% reduction of the 2006/07 baseline	Within and outside	Climate change, society and savings	Yes	
305–5 Reduction of GHG emissions kgCO$_2$	31% reduction on 2006/07 baseline	Within and outside	Climate change, society and savings	Yes	
411–1 Indigenous people human rights MM5 and MM6 (Mining and Metals Sector Disclosure)	All sites	Within and outside	Building strong relationships and respecting human rights	Yes	
304–2 Significant impacts of activities, products and services on biodiversity	All sites by 2015 – a full suite of appropriate biodiversity management plans (BMPs) in place	Within	Responsible stewardship	Yes	

And now for the bombshell! Upon coming to understand the framework, you may have noticed the following:

1   It is possible to produce a GRI Standards compliant report without disclosing any material topics. It may just be possible if your business is not selling anything and does not use resources. However, this would have to be evidenced as the result of a stakeholder engagement that did not identify any material issues.
2   It is possible to provide minimal information in the Standard Disclosure requests for information. However, the premise that a report should be a useful tool to support meaningful dialogue means that a mature, accurate and concise approach is needed. Interesting, engaging and quality reports are the best.
3   It is possible to produce a GRI Standards compliant report identifying the material topics but omitting the provision of quantitative or qualitative data by stating that information is not available. (We discuss omissions later in greater detail in Chapter 6.) Essentially, omissions refers to when an organisation declines to present the data required from what the process has identified as being a material issue(s). GRI allows omissions within certain parameters, provided the organisation explains its strategy to monitor, track and report the data in the future. However, GRI reserves the right to deem a report not 'in accordance' if it has significant omissions.

Though it is technically possible to submit such a report, it is not desirable and may indicate an abuse of the flexibility the guidance offers. Bluffing in sustainability amounts to 'fooling oneself' and losing out on the process benefits and meaningful strategic benefits. Now we are sure this is obvious, but with this book, you do not need such loopholes, as it is easier and a lot less scary to just do it right.

6 Report

The writing of a sustainability report requires discipline and creativity; remember, it is a public document and should hold meticulously accurate qualitative and quantitative information. The report should be a consise communication on how the organisation creates value in the short, medium and long term.

This chapter will describe the key areas to clarify what is needed in a report and where help to make report writing automated can be found.

Before diving into the report writing process, think about which communication method is best for each group of stakeholders, and what size budget was identified when reporting was approved by the board. Various mediums are used to back up the written report. We have found cartoons to be a great approach to increasing both the size and the interest of the audience. The Heinekin spoken word video sustainability report 'Let's Get Frank', went viral in 2016 (https://secure.theheinekencompany.com/latest-report). We have also found audio reports, video reports and so on. The method of communication may affect who is involved, the lead-in times they need and the structure of the report. It is preferable to be able to access the entire sustainability reporting information as a single output or publication in one place, but having multiple platforms, especially in this time of social media, can make the report more accessible to a wider audience. Consistency across the channels of reporting is also important, as well as authenticity and being true to the ten principles that guide the report's content and quality.

There may be a big difference in the communication methods chosen for internal stakeholders compared to external stakeholders. Internal stakeholders will be easier to reach out to, and more informal methods like emails, posters, team meetings, memos, coffee mornings and notice boards can be used. External stakeholders can be informed and communicated with by press release, conferences, trade shows, stakeholder meetings, organisational and sustainability report websites and across the platforms identified in Diagram 5.

Schedule 6 Report Phase Timeline

	December					January				February				March					April			
	2	9	16	23	30	7	14	21	28	4	11	18	25	1	8	15	22	29	6	13	20	27
REPORT (Review)																						
20 Develop narrative for statement	▓	▓	▓	▓	▓	▓	▓	▓	▓	▓	▓	▓	▓									
21 Draft sustainability/integrated report	▓	▓	▓	▓	▓	▓	▓	▓	▓	▓	▓	▓	▓									
22 Regular progress meetings				▓							▓		▓									
23 GRI application level check														▓	▓							
24 Finalise the report																	▓	▓				
25 Send for publication																			▓			
26 Launch report																				▓		
27 Feedback																						▓

The Report phase is a very distinct phase in the reporting cycle, typically taking three or four months from starting to write the narrative to getting it GRI checked, if an organisation chooses this route. The Report phase may also include publication to various media, launch and the positioning of mechanisms to receive and respond to feedback. The timetable for writting the report can be seen in Schedule 6.

The report should be written with accessibility for stakeholders in mind and ensuring that the specific report meets readers' needs for key and critical information. The report is typically written and coordinated by the lead sustainability Coordinator to reflect the strategy, values, brand, character and personality of the organisation. Any comparable corporate report would usually be drafted and shared with the directors, board and senior managers as part of good governance, ensuring that the report is interesting, understandable, balanced and easy to follow; this should also be the case with your sustainability report.

Template 4 provides the basic contents of a report.

Template 4 Sustainability Report Contents Table

Cover page

Contents table

Foreword

Corporate details and placeholder for 'Materiality Matters' icon, if applicable

About the report and boundary and feedback 1

Statement from the CEO/Chair 2

Introduction and performance highlights 3

Key themes 4

Material topics matrix 5

Stakeholder engagement – identification and prioritisation. 6

General disclosures 7

Topic-specific disclosures – topics and management approach 8

Claim – Core/Comprehensive 9

Financial performance 10

Assurance 11

GRI content index (placeholder for GRI check) 12

Closing page

Appendices (may have links to management accounts, directors' statement, strategic report and so on)

Many of the sections are self-explanatory and well detailed in corresponding sections of this book; however, a couple of sections would benefit from a brief explanation.

The 'About the report' section is the opportunity to 'tell the organisation's story', explaining why the report is titled/themed the way it is. State the business model and remember the key reporting objectives of conciseness, strategic focus, credibility and ease of navigation. The section also states the 'in accordance' option, any Sector Disclosures used and the type of report (sustainability/integrated/referenced). It should provide a brief outline narrative about material topics, the report history and the report period. It should also give a brief insight on the organisation's key sustainability statistics (i.e. turnover, profit, CO_2 emissions, water and waste to landfill). Organisations that do this well use infographics to quickly convey their key areas of performance.

The chapter on 'Key themes' is the area of the report where the organisation can build on the discussion of the business model that may have been started in 'About the report'. It enables companies to state their products, strategic tools and values that encapsulate their sustainability performance; an example includes Marks & Spencer's Plan A sustainability report.

The chapter on 'Where we can improve' is an excellent vehicle for you to identify and discuss material topics where performance can be improved. This section is good for the credibility of your report as it supports balanced reporting and respects the position that an organisation is not perfect but can provide stakeholders with simple access to critical information.

The layout of the report will often follow organisational preference and bear in mind the need for corporate branding. A top tip which Total Eco Management was the first to do was to flag the Disclosure Reference Number in the instrument being reported against, next to relevant text in the sustainability report. It means report writing needs to be more disciplined, but the added focus makes the report much easier and clearer to read for stakeholders and faster to navigate and find the areas on which a discerning stakeholder wants to focus.

Another issue regards the length of the report. Under 50 pages is preferable, but certainly try to avoid exceeding 100 pages. A concise report is preferred because it is easier to find the relevant points and should be easier and quicker to read.

At this time, there are few GRI Standards sustainability reports and even fewer integrated reports following the new International Integrated Reporting Framework. An example of a good report is of great value to organisations, so you should look for good examples emerging in your sector on the international GRI Sustainability Disclosure Database: http://database.globalreporting.org/.

Develop narrative for most senior person's statement

This statement is written by the CEO or most senior person at the organisation. This is a balanced statement identifying performance, the organisation's relationship to the Sustainable Development Goals, the type of report (sustainability or integrated), progress, achievement, near misses and failed targets that could be learnt from for corporate improvement. It provides a concise picture of sustainability impacts, actions and interests. According to research by Corporate Register, the inclusion of bad news was cited as one of the most significant credibility builders for report readers.

The statement should talk of the value reporting brings to the organisation, any integration of financial and natural capital from sustainable operations, trends on climate change, emissions, human rights and other key impacts the organisation has. It may also mention key awards, corporate risks and responsibilities, and outline leadership topics. It is important not to lose sight of the key purposes of reporting: being able to drive change, respond to global, national, regional and local issues, and create a better society through protecting scarce resourses, reducing poverty and reporting transparently to bring about a sustainable global economy.

The statement should relate to the main report. It should promote balance and may consider impact(s) where performance has not been so good and where actions to improve have already taken place. The report is often signed, and a photograph of the most senior person is incorporated.

Company accreditations

GRI embraces the qualitative and quantitative requirements of many of the world's more significant environmental social governance standards; indeed, GRI has formal MOUs and partners with many other standards, enabling a reporter to use GRI yet cover the bases to report to these other standards due to its reporting requirement alignment. However, though there is common ground, harmonisation does not extend to consistency of formats or submission requirements. Consequently, the reality is that companies must decide on the data they want to report relative to each framework demanding the data. But it certainly helps to have harmonised metrics because the end reports for each standard can carry and discuss the same data. It is usual for respective reports to indicate any other standards to which the reporting organisation responds.

How do GRI Standards relate to other environmental and sustainability standards? GRI has formal 'linkage documents' which provide guidance for using GRI reporting in combination with other standards such as IIRC, the Carbon Disclosure Project (CDP), the ISO Standards, the UN

Global Compact, the UK Mandatory GHG Reporting 2013, and the Organisation for Economic Cooperation and Development (OECD); it also links with the EU Non-Financial Directive. In addition, emerging governmental and global regulations and stock exchanges reference GRI as a compliant methodology.

The Declaration

A defining factor of a GRI report is its claim. A GRI Standards report must state the 'in accordance' option as Core or Comprehensive, for example:

> We declare this report has been prepared in accordance with the GRI Standards: Core option.

Or

> We declare this report has been prepared in accordance with the GRI Standards: Comprehensive option.

Or

> This report is GRI referenced and contains disclosures from the GRI Standards as specifically identified for social, economic and environmental topics, including the management approach'.

If the report is also an integrated report and complies with the International IR Framework, it should also state, 'This report is in accordance with the International IR Framework'.

Draft sustainability/integrated report

We advocate that report writting should be built and developed across a set reporting period (i.e. fiscal year or calendar year). This makes the management of achieving the draft and final report easier.

This is an important step in the process because, once the draft report is completed, it can be checked by Total Eco Management for how well it aligns with the GRI Standards. Disclosure Review Service, Content Index Service, Materiality Disclosures Service and SDG Mapping Service checks are also provided by GRI.

Content index

Not all sustainability reporting standards have a requirement for a content index, so this might not be relevant to some report writers. If the content index is applicable, it is typically located at the end of the report. The lead sustainability coordinator should manage the completion of the index and coordinate the Sustainability Team to provide and possibly enter the data. You can do this when the sustainability report text is nearing its final draft. The Total Eco Management software outlined in Chapter 7 automates the completion of the content index as a navigation tool for the sustainability/ integrated report.

The content index is a rarely written about area. As a navigation tool, it is capable of imparting raw information quickly on which GRI disclosures have been made and where they can be found.

The content index lists the disclosures in a table format that is required to include:

- The title and publication year for each of the GRI Standards used.
- The GRI number and title for each disclosure made.
- The page number(s) and/or URL(s) for each disclosure for transparency on where the information can be found, either within the report or in other published materials.
- Applicable omissions and, where permitted, the reason(s) for omission when a required disclosure cannot be made.
- A statement on whether the item is assured.
- A statement with the 'in accordance' option in its heading (i.e. 'In accordance: Core option', or 'In accordance: Comprehensive option'), Or if it is GRI referenced.

Template 5 shows the information and format of a compliant content index.

Template 5 Content Index

GRI Content Index				
In accordance (Core option/Comprehensive option) or GRI referenced				
GRI Standard [include the title and publication year for each of the GRI Standards used to prepare the report]	**Disclosure** [include the number and title for each disclosure mode]	**Page number(s) and/ or URL(s)**	**Omission** [see GRI 101: Foundation for information on reasons for omission]	**Assured** [yes/no]
GRI 101: Foundation 2016 [GRI 101 does not include any disclosures]				
General Disclosures [the list of general disclosures mode, based on whether the report has been prepared in accordance with the Core or Comprehensive option]				
GRI 102: General Disclosures 2016	102–1 Name of the organisation	Page 3	[this disclosure cannot be omitted]	
	102–2 Activities, brands, products and services	Page 4–5 and website [direct hyperlink]	[this disclosure cannot be omitted]	
Material Topics [the list of material topics included in the report, as reported in Disclosure 102–47. The reporting organisation is required to include any material topics reported on which are not covered by the GRI Standards]				
Emissions [example of topic covered by the topic-specific standards]				
GRI 103: Management Approach 2016	103–1 Explanation of the material topic and its boundaries	Page 20	[this disclosure cannot be omitted]	
	103–2 The management approach and its components	Page 21	–	

(Continued)

(Continued)

GRI 305: Emissions 2016	305–1 Direct (Scope 1) GHG emissions	Page 22	—	☑
	305–2 Energy indirect (Scope 2) GHG emissions	" "	Information unavailable for 305–2 [description of the steps being taken to obtain the data and the expected timeframe for doing so]	☑
Freedom of Speech [example of topic covered by the topic-specific standards]				
GRI 103: Management Approach 2016	103–1 Explanation of the material topic and its boundaries	Page 28	[this disclosure cannot be omitted]	
	103–2 The management approach and its components	Page 29	—	
	[title of topic-specific disclosure]	Page 30	—	
[not applicable if the material topic is not covered by an existing GRI Standard; it is recommended, but not required, to report other appropriate disclosures]				

Omissions

An omission has a specific response:

1 Not Applicable (i.e. it is not a relevant disclosure to the organisation)
2 Specific Legal Prohibitions (i.e. the law does not allow the matter to be disclosed)
3 Unavailable (i.e. full or partial information appertaining to the disclosure is not available)
4 Specific Confidential Constraints (i.e. the information is proprietary and would reveal, say, a commercial edge)

Omissions, where applicable, must be explained: you should state the reason for the omission and when the information will be provided.

It should be noted that too many omissions may void the claim made on a report by the organisation (i.e. the report not being an 'in accordance' report as stated in the claim).

Completing the content index is best achieved by simple and direct responses, so you should try to keep responses short.

Similarly, when completing the disclosures on the management approach, every effort should be made to keep the response concise. To avoid an unnecessary narrative where an organisational policy covers multiple material topics (i.e. if an organisation has an environmental policy that covers materials, energy, water and emissions, a single response covering all of these topics can be provided). Some reporters have been found to make the mistake of not reconciling the text in the report to the content index, so care is needed when nearing publication to ensure that the two are fully cross-referenced.

GRI report-checking services

The purpose of the GRI checking service is to check whether a report is in accordance with the GRI's sustainability reporting guidelines. Verifying the quality of the reported information and the process of preparing the disclosures is beyond the scope of this service. The service is offered for free to GRI Gold Community members.

An organisation can choose whether or not to have their report checked by GRI. A successful check results in GRI issuing an icon for the relevant check, which can be placed at the head of the content index.

Five types of report checking are offered as GRI services:

1 Disclosure Review Service – A review of the specific disclosures to address an organisation's approach to stakeholder engagement and materiality assessment.

2   Content Index Service – Improves the accuracy and usability of an organisation's GRI content index and ensure alignment with the GRI Standards.
3   Materiality Disclosure Service – Materiality information is the heart of sustainability reporting. This service confirms that the disclosures related to materiality are correctly located in the GRI content index and in the text of the final report.
4   SDG Mapping Service – Gives internal and external stakeholders more faith and trust, where GRI confirms whether the Sustainable Development Goals have been correctly mapped against the GRI disclosures.
5   GRI Referenced Service – This is for reporters who do not use the GRI Standards in their entirety to report and use the claim that they are 'GRI referenced'. GRI checks whether the claim is transparent and aligned with the GRI Standards.

GRI makes clear to the users of these services by way of a disclaimer that GRI does not verify, check or pass judgement on the quality of disclosures within the report, as that responsibility remains with the reporting organisation. GRI services are also not an external assurance engagement, although the service is complementary to such engagements. GRI does not carry any legal responsibility for the implementation of feedback.

A good time to send a report for checking is once the report reaches final report stage, post assurance, but before it goes to publication. This is because GRI's check is likely to lead to amendments to the report.

In order to conduct the 'check', GRI requires the organisation to send the following (to reportservices@globalreporting.org):

1   Draft sustainability/integrated report and associated links
2   Content index with cross-referenced links to 1
3   Sign-up form

Software is one easy way to respond to a GRI check because it provides all of the information in the ideal format for a report check. There will be more on software in Chapter 7.

It is a good practice to call GRI in advance to check the time they require to provide a response which varies at different time of the year. Contact with GRI is a helpful part of the process as GRI likes to have a dialogue with organisations before the report is published.

GRI's response can be very thorough, leading to many amendments which may include having to re-align links. GRI then carries out further checks by repeating the process on the organisation's amended report, and this may be further repeated until GRI Reporting Services are satisfied.

Finalise report and send for publication

Once GRI is satisfied, it will issue the relevant report-checking icon and certification statement.

The icon can be copied into the final version of the report by the publisher, and, at this time, the reporting organisation can incorporate the elements of a final report, including photos, infographics, page colour coding, branding and so on.

Launch report

Use a wide range of platforms to launch the report. It is useful to register it on the Corporate Register Database and directly on GRI's Sustainability Disclosure Database.

As an example, Total Eco Management's integrated report is on the our TEM website to view as an e-book, chosen for the extra enjoyment and interaction it provides to the reader and stakeholder. It is also in a PDF format. It is registered as an integrated report on the GRI Sustainability Disclosure Database and the Corporate Register Database.

TEM's integrated report had the additional task of showcasing the International IR Reporting Framework so that any reporter can easily discern what a quality integrated report should look like and use this to both understand the constituents of an integrated report and make their own reporting easier. Bearing in mind that it is produced by experts in GRI, it has helped many and is one of the more popular pages of our website. You can view it here: www.totalecomanagement.co.uk/report.html. If you go to it, please feel free to comment at kye@temltd.co.uk; all comments are welcomed and all will receive a response.

Remember, reporting is essential to modern business whether the organisation is large, small, multinational, public, private, voluntary, charitable, governmental or non-governmental. No matter what the description of your company, the lesson for management and boards is 'If you are not reporting, your competitors and peers almost surely are'. The task of 'catching up' will only grow larger. So now is the time to get started!

Your report launch is an important moment for all involved in the process and also for your stakeholders. It is time to recognise the help of all involved and reflect on what has been learned and how the organisation is contributing to a sustainable future. Some organisations have been known to award/recognise those who were particularly helpful during the reporting process, which in turn can increase employee enthusiasm and commitment to sustainability.

Feedback

Gathering external and internal feedback of lessons learnt is the first step to prepare for the next reporting period. This can be done in many ways. It could be as simple as asking a few questions to colleagues, or sending around a survey, or conducting short face-to-face interviews, or running focus group meetings. Questions can include 'Which activities worked well?', 'What went wrong and why?', 'How can we develop our strengths for the next report?' and 'What needs to be changed within our organisation to facilitate better reporting?'

Feedback is an ongoing process; information gathered should be part of the review process to be included in the next reporting period. The review focuses on the topics that were material in the previous reporting period and also considers stakeholder feedback. The findings can be used as a point of reference in the Prepare and Connect phases, an 'identification' step for the next reporting cycle, where you continue engaging with stakeholders.

The sustainability report itself should have a section requesting feedback and, where possible, the organisation should record and respond to any stakeholder feedback recieved. Some companies offer prizes to encourage greater stakeholder responses (e.g. responses go into a draw to win, say, a 'green phone').

As part of the feedback, you can ask internal and external stakeholders what their preference is for the style of report communication in an effort to source ideas to improve future report communications.

Feedback leads neatly into the next reporting cycle, and you seamlessly begin the process again. In governance terms, the CEO might produce an information update report for the board based on the feedback information. From this board report, the cycle can start again, beginning with the Prepare phase Development Plan and kick-off meeting. The good news for first-time reporters is that the second time is much easier than the first.

Many reporters engage Total Eco Management to assess their reports for compliance, constructive praise to build on what's good and areas for improvement, but also comparability with peers and best practices. This service is ideal because it guides organisations on how their report can be improved currently or for the next reporting cycle.

Remember, sustainability reporting is a living process and does not begin or end with a publication or a communication. Some of our more mature reporters reflect on their first year as being brilliant for the organisation, but it was only when they got to year three that the wider consequences and benefits became more apparent, and the reporting process became a habit, part and parcel of the organisation's everyday life, and, like most habits, it then becomes a driver to ever-continuous improvement that is fundamental to a sustainable future.

7 Software

An increasing element of our working environment is about smart phones, apps and the cloud, which are making life easier and more productive at an individual and corporate level.

It is hardly a revelation to conclude that sustainability reporting is becoming a central part of communicating organisational annual performance. Software that supports this process is also increasingly essential; it is a system that does not detract but helps build a firm foundation for sustainability alongside the focus on the material, whilst producing outputs of gold standard report documentation that supports regulatory compliance.

There is increasing recognition that reporting organisations need software to support the reporting process and data collection. Also organisations are reporting via apps and mobile support software.

As you can appreciate, the report has to be produced first, and there is software that helps the report production, then assembles the information into the pages and information required for an organisation's sustainability report and content index. In addition, the software provides templates to assist the organisation through all of the phases and interactions involved in the reporting process, as detailed throughout this book, through setting out the business case to preparing for the process and engaging with stakeholders, to identifying material topics and boundaries, as well as templates for data collection with responsible person(s), all wrapped up in a secure setting able to be accessed by authorised personnel from anywhere in the world. The name of this tool is SRT (Sustainability Reporting Tool), produced by sustainability experts Total Eco Management: www.totalecomanagement.co.uk. The G4 version was GRI-certified software; partners are being sought for a GRI Standards form of this unique and much needed SRT software. Get in touch if you want to be involved.

SRT significantly speeds up the reporting process and provides confidence to the reporting organisation and its stakeholders, ensuring that there is a good understanding of how and what to report. It provides reassurance that an organisation's report is achieving a level of GRI compliance, or is at least on a competent reporting path that is robust for sustainability report delivery but futureproofed for seamless delivery of gold standard GRI reports.

SRT facilitates the process of reporting from linking sustainability context and strategy in the preparatory kick-off meeting to connecting to stakeholders, defining materiality and relevance, monitoring and report production. It enables an organisation to report as an ongoing and continuous process. SRT contains step-by-step guidance for the systems' use; it has links to GRI Standards online, social media connection opportunities and messaging. SRT has been designed so that in time an organisation can generate more integrated reports.

Software can help organisations compensate for gaps in experience and knowledge whilst easing some of the negative experiences of reporting, such as the need for endless patience, as it covers the whole process around which some organisations appoint multiple consultants.

8 Assurance

Assurance is about the independent verification of sustainability report content and data for stakeholders. It further provides insight and guidance to the reporting organisation. KPMG's Survey of Corporate Sustainability Reporting 2017 found that 67% and rising of the Fortune 250, the largest companies, assure their sustainability reports. In 2013 the figure was 59%; the 8% rise evidences larger companies seeing value in promoting the reliability of their information.

Cutting straight to the chase, at GRI Standards 102–56, external assurance of sustainability reports is recommended and advised, in addition to any internal assurance checks. Like the KPMG findings, GRI is seeing incidences of assurance steadily growing as interest in sustainability reporting grows among investors and other stakeholders.

The assurer should be independent of the reporting organisation and demonstrably competent in the requirements of reporting standards and the sector in which the reporting organisation works. Assurance requires the identification of exactly what disclosures the assurer has assured so that stakeholders can be clear on exactly how much of a report is actually assured. A recognised assurance standard should be used, such as Account-Ability's AA1000 or ISAE3000, with a final written report, and its opinions and conclusions being publicly available.

One of the author's expert hats is as a sustainability expert and an AccountAbility Lead Certified Sustainability Assurance Practitioner CSAP. We strongly value your work with organisations globally to verify the integration of the core principles of the AA1000 Standards.

External assurance can greatly enhance the credibility of sustainability disclosures because it helps to build confidence in the reported information and build relationships of trust. Investors, rating agencies and other analysts increasingly look for assurance when making investment and rating decisions based on sustainability performance. For example, issues such as carbon risk and the ability to trade emissions may have direct financial implications. Generally, assurance or verification involves a systematic, independent and documented process for the evaluation of reported sustainability information against pre-defined criteria or benchmarks and, in some cases, according to an assurance or verification standard.

Perhaps the most commonly used assurance standard is the Accountability AA1000AS Standard. It assures sustainability by assessing the principles an organisation has followed and the levels of detail and quality of the data. Type 1 Assurance will only assess the reporting principles: materiality, stakeholder inclusivity and responsiveness. Type 2 Assurance is better because it looks at the data. The level of detail for the assurance can be 'moderate', requiring specific evidence per material item. Or it can be 'high', requiring a thorough assessment of the information, people and reporting processes and data at many of the organisation's installations across the world.

Assurance is generally carried out by a multidisciplinary team, and for many large multinational enterprises (MNEs), it is an 18-week (on average) process that feeds into the final draft of the reporting process prior to the GRI report-checking services (see Chapter 6).

The assurance typically involves careful planning, followed by work to look at the scope of reporting, interviews with management and an early draft review of findings. Thereafter, there will be stakeholder reviews, documentation reviews, alternative source checking, operational interviews and site visits, data triangulation checks, assurance claim checking and then the Assurance Team has a calibration meeting to assess the situation thus far. Thereafter, a verification of further data for completeness may be made, then a draft report for management and a draft assurance report will be produced. This is a great opportunity for constructive dialogue and learning, which has huge value when done with competent assurers knowledgeable of your business sector and GRI/IR. The final stage is a completed assurance report signed off on by a lead sustainability assurance practitioner or similar.

A range of different providers, including accountants and specialist consultants, can provide external assurance or verification of sustainability reports. Providers are governed by different codes of conduct or standards, depending upon their affiliation.

There has been a paradigm shift for assurers with respect to reporting suppliers and material topics. In the role of a qualified lead assurance practitioner, we look for reporters to be able to evidence their processes to report, actions against the same, flow of information data, compliance with procedures, and outcome, often interrogating environmental health and safety management systems and checking any media reports on past and recent failures. The main issue we would seek to assure is whether the report meets the 'in accordance' criteria. Does the list of material topics make sense?

We appreciate that, if stakeholders cannot trust sustainability reports, then their value will be limited. Internal audits can be used to add great value to sustainability management, so organisations should be encouraged to do this.

GRI Standards identifies seven qualities for the external assurance of reports. External assurance providers should:

- Be independent from the reporting organisation and therefore able to reach and publish an objective and impartial opinion or conclusion on the report;
- Be demonstrably competent in the subject matter and assurance practices;
- Apply quality control procedures to the assurance engagement;
- Conduct the engagement in a manner that is systematic, documented, evidence-based and characterised by defined procedures;
- Assess whether the report provides a reasonable and balanced presentation of performance, taking into consideration the veracity of data in the report as well as the overall selection of content;
- Assess the extent to which the report preparer has applied the GRI Standards in the course of reaching its conclusions;
- Issue a written report that is publicly available and includes an opinion or set of conclusions, a description of the responsibilities of the report preparer and the assurance providers and a summary of the work performed to explain the nature of the assurance conveyed by the assurance report.

It should be noted that an assurance is not the same as an audit, and the people who carry out each should be quite separate and independent. An audit is a systematic examination or verification of an organisation's books of account against specific criteria by qualified accountants, using accounting standards in the case of a financial statement audit and/or organisational policies and procedures in the case of other internal or external audits.

9 Additional insights for reporters and non-reporters

Integrated reporting

In this section we provide a first-hand account of the development of the International Reporting (IR) Framework, as we were representatives on the pilot programme. The pilot programme that developed the framework was comprised of over 80 leading multinationals such as Microsoft, HSBC, Marks & Spencer, Unilever, Samsung, Coca-Cola and NHS. The KPMG Survey on Corporate Reporting 2017 states that only 3% of reports are integrated and reference the IIRC.

At the outset, the objective was to create a corporate narrative standard that would connect corporate activities and finances to the impacts and consequences of organisations to the natural world. 'The natural environment is essential for humanity to survive and thrive', a position we presented for a global GRI webinar on biodiversity.

Originally, an IR was to be a single report covering sustainability and financial issues and providing a 21st century replacement for management accounts. IR was needed so that an organisation's response to sustainability and long-term value creation could be understood and was transparently disclosed to any stakeholder who needed to know. The report was to be concise and reflective of an organisation's business model. It was certainly the case that the report would be a fine display of connectivity, making clear linkages and impacts between the financial and sustainable parts (e.g. if energy is material, it is seamlessly linked to climate change and cost to clarify the impact of energy conservation and show the value behind the organisation's energy strategy with its risks and opportunities).

However, from the outset the big financial houses and investors had the greatest influence in the development process and the outcome of the International IR Framework; for some, it is significantly short of the original intention. The framework's three-month global consultation elicited 350 responses. This is very few considering the scale of the organisations involved in its development, many of which employ tens of thousands of people; M&S alone employs 81,000 people. Put another way, it averages less than 15 responses per country of the 25 countries the IIRC has set to trial the framework. Not all of the responses to the consultation were supportive, and the world is observing progress with interest. Perhaps the few responses are indicative of the level of interest, where GRI retains the leading position for guidance to produce a report, meeting the original objectives of integrated reporting. By comparison, GRI consultations attract thousands of responses.

When an integrated report incorporates GRI, it can provide a coherent understanding on how organisations create and sustain value into the future. Prince Charles explained in his address to launch the IR Framework at the end of 2013 that the framework supports a transformation in corporate reporting to improve communication on the impacts and consequences of our actions on natural capital through more integrated thinking. In the 21st century, what the world needs is urgent and rapid impact reduction for the planet and society, and good profitable business performance.

The International Integrated Reporting Council (IIRC) is a coalition led mainly by finance houses and investors. The reporting established by the International IR Framework focuses on organisational value and the capitals (resources and relationships as stock of value that are increased, decreased and transformed through the organisation's activities, i.e. intellectual, financial, manufactured, social and relationships, and natural capital; see the Glossary for a detailed explanation of capital). IR seeks to embed integrated thinking into mainstream public and private business practices. It is another framework making corporate provision for global sustainability and economic stability.

For clarity, the International IR Framework definition of an integrated report, on page 7, 'is a concise communication about how an organisations' strategy, governance, performance and prospects, in the context of its external environment, lead to the creation of value over the short, medium, and long term'. It does allow omissions of these principles by its reporting organisations.

The IIRC Framework provides principles-based guidance for organisations to deliver a corporate narrative report based on the principles of:

- Connectivity of Information
- Business Model
- Strategic Focus and Future Orientation
- Stakeholder Relationships
- Conciseness
- Materiality

The IIRC does not prescribe any specific performance topics, methods of measuring or disclosures of individual matters. But it does specifically require:

1   A statement from the organisation's lead in governance
2   Acknowledgement that this was a collective decision of the governance team
3   A conclusion that the report is in accordance with the IR Framework

The three items mentioned are required before a report can be said to be 'in accordance' with the International IR Framework. The report should be written by the directors and can stand alone or be part of an existing compliance report. The guidance specifically mentions that the IR can be a summary of the financial statement or sustainability report, and can be part of an organisation's website. Interestingly, the IR requests comparability in spite of not having clear measures to manage or targets to achieve.

The framework mentions 'application of generally accepted measurement and disclosures methods as appropriate'. This includes use with GRI, but again, because an organisation can choose whatever standard they want or not, the IR Framework could suffer over time from comparing apples to pears.

The IIRC signed an MOU with GRI in the early part of 2013 for the purpose of harmonising with one another; however, by the end of 2013, the final IIRC Framework failed to mention GRI even once. In a world of increasing collaboration, the IIRC's approach runs contrary to any best business practice.

Even a tertiary glance at the International IR Framework reveals that it provides less than what the GRI Standards already provide. In the view of many, using the IR Guidance without the GRI Standards will produce a far-from-robust report. We predict that this is likely to be a future source of problems, where organisations claim to have produced an IR report but fail to identify and prioritise stakeholder engagement, materiality, supply chain boundaries, performance scope, and so on.

The IR also has a developed world feel which may reflect a focus on Western interests. It is also clear that the IR report is targeted at investors and their needs and interests, which are also often focused on OECD interests (i.e. where global wealth continues to grow, increasing the gap between the rich and the poor). The IR seems to lack diversity, inclusion and the interest of large areas of Africa, Asia and South America and the problems faced in these regions.

Actually, it is quite possible to produce an integrated report using GRI alone. Essentially, the requirements of the IR Framework could be achieved through the simple embellishment of GRI strategy and analysis, GRI Standards 1–2, with some extended discussion on capital and a claim of compliance.

So, it is shocking to note the HSBC's IR report is hundreds of pages long, with many other organisations also failing the IR Framework principle of achieving brief reports. However, early GRI Standards reports are displaying positive signs of being increasingly more concise and disciplined.

The IIRC also has no checking process for reports or assurance requirements to assure stakeholders on the credibility of the report or the trust the reports have gained. The IIRC's use of concepts that are not understood will lead to confusion, inconsistency and lack of legitimacy as to what the report is seeking to achieve; however, this can be overcome with training, as TEM already provides GRI-certified training partners. TEM used GRI to underpin one of the first concise integrated reports using the IIRC guidelines and framework; the report was GRI application level, checked by GRI directly and assessed as an integrated report. TEM's report serves as a great example of an integrated report with sustainability at its heart and can be viewed on both the GRI Sustainability Disclosure Database and TEM's database of GRI sustainability reports. In addition, TEM has worked with others to produce a GRI integrated report, including a construction institution with a multidisciplinary membership of professionals and experts across 126 countries.

The 'I' in IR should stand for 'investor' because the framework is actually requiring an 'investor report'. The IIRC has chosen to focus on listed companies and the production of a report for the investor community. The IIRC has acknowledged the default position of using their framework in the production of two or more reports, being one report for the investor and another for stakeholders. This detracts from the original intention of a single report and indeed the principles already established for an integrated report by King III, the leading global legislation from South Africa on integrated reporting, and GRI.

So, the bombshell is that the IIRC becomes a mis-description, but that's a debate for another day. This in itself makes the IR Framework unsustainable for organisations that continue to seek the single-report solution that is inclusive of all businesses, where 93% of businesses that are categorised as large, SME and smaller, this is a huge chunk of business to have missed out. In short, what the IIRC hailed as a crisis will have been wasted.

Broadly, a single, proper integrated report is still the way forward, provided it has sustainability reporting using GRI or similar at its heart. A book titled *Understanding Integrated Reporting*, published by Routledge, agrees; on page 31 it says, 'GRI is a pre-requisite for IR'. Both are reinforced by the research in KPMG's 2017 survey, which makes clear that only a few organisations do integrated reporting, and even fewer do it well; however, for IR to have credibility, it should incorporate GRI.

The bad practice of organisations doing integrated reports without GRI is likely to be detrimental to those organisations as they get 'outed' by stakeholders as unacceptable 'greenwashers'.

10 Q&A for reporters and non-reporters

Who is GRI? GRI is a collaboration and a public for good, seeking to generate a sustainable global economy. Over the past 21 years, GRI has evolved as a common and consistent framework where organisations are free to choose those elements that are material. GRI is keen for organisations to train and upgrade from G4 to the new GRI Standards as soon as possible.

When did GRI Standards reporting start and G4 reporting cease? This occurred on 1st July 2018 and 30th June 2018, respectively, for all organisations.

Who should report to GRI Standards? All organisations should report: MNEs, 'brands', SMEs, voluntary, charitable, private and public organisations; there are even many micro organisations that report. A common factor in reporters is a culture that seeks to improve society in the long term. Suppliers and SMEs working with large companies also report.

What knowledge is needed? Knowledge of corporate sustainability reporting, leadership, governance and metrics data management are needed. However, good advice is to get the right support and guidance when starting out from people who know how to use the GRI Standards. This is important because reporting should never be a tick-box exercise; reporting is a tool for change, conveying your story and your message.

Why are there good and bad reports? The key reason why the range of reports varies from the sloppy to high-degree adherence is generally because the corporate sustainability profession is young and is evolving in governance and management competencies. However, this book is a step-by-step guide to raise the bar by exampling good reporting policies and practices.

Care is needed at this time, as there are a growing number of reporters producing integrated reports that do not comply with either the GRI or the IIRC. The lack of knowledge and direction in this area has left it wide open to abuse; however, it is highlighting those who do not understand sustainability as a core discipline and must understand that, without sustainability skills, they cannot evidence how their business model creates and sustains value, and that could make them uninvestable.

Where can one access examples of reports? Visit the GRI Sustainability Disclosure Database: www.globalreporting.org.

What is the cost to report? The cost of issuing a sustainability report may vary in the same way as it does for producing management accounts. Many elements contribute to the cost, including data collection, report preparation and publishing costs, external assurance and costs associated with implementing new processes, including staff training, consultancy, IT systems and so on. For example, a study on the costs of compliance with the Danish Financial Statements Act estimated the cost of publication to be between €871 and €43,830 per business, depending on the chosen type of report. The EU estimates compliance with its Non-Financial Reporting Directive to be less than €5,000 a year.

Does reporting provide any benefit to organisations? Organisations that disclose are best positioned to manage their environmental impact risks and opportunities. Many studies have demonstrated the value of reporting, evidencing how reputation and brand are enhanced, risks and costs are reduced, income is enhanced, attracting investment capital is easier and costs less, and compliance with legislation is improved, along with staff attraction and retention. PWC and Deutsche Bank studies confirm the cost of capital reduction to reporting organisations. Leaders understand that there is no conflict between resource conservation and profit. This is an important point because being sustainable advances humanity; sustainable technologies seamlessly enable people to enjoy the same things they always have but in a way that is less harmful to the planet.

Do many places mandate reporting? Companies are reporting out of the need to compete, business failure and the need to respond and stay in business, and, of course, legislative shift. The European Commission accounting legislation will soon mandate the reporting of environmental social governance for up to 18,000 large companies, placing Europe in a leadership position on corporate accountability. In addition, 44 stock exchanges and rising require all their listed companies to produce a sustainability report. Fifty-six governments and rising have requirements for organisations to report, including Australia, China, Denmark, Austria, the Netherlands, Finland, Belgium, France, India, Germany, Norway, Spain, Sweden and the United States (amongst others) (CDSB and GRI). Carrot and Sticks has developed governmental policy initiatives and regulations to promote sustainability reporting and/or ESG disclosure. The European Commission has adopted resolutions and proposed amendments to council directives for enhancing the transparency of certain companies on social and environmental matters. In the UK, the Mandatory Reporting Guidance,

April 2013, sets GRI as a recommended methodology. Reporting is here and spreading, so companies need to get involved or risk being left behind by their peers who understand the importance of sustainability to economies.

Ten stock exchanges across Asia, South America, Europe, the US, Japan, the UK and South Africa require listed organisations to disclose their sustainability across ESG (environmental, social and governance) areas (Verdantix Report – Benchmark on Non-Financial Reporting Rules 2012; 95% of the global top 250 sustainability report, CDSB). Over 75% of the world's largest 4000 companies report. Over 80% of those reporting use the GRI guidelines.

How does one know when one is looking at a GRI Standards report? The report must state the 'in accordance' Core option or Comprehensive option (i.e. 'This report has been prepared in accordance with the GRI Standards: Core option'). The report must contain a content index which acts as the report specification. Materiality should be immediately apparent as a key focus. There should be considerable details about stakeholder engagement in the process of identifying and defining the selected material content and where it matters in relation to boundary, either as direct or indirect contributions, or indeed both. (e.g. carbon dioxide emissions are relevant to the reporting organisation but also the wider impact of its activity with its supply chain). The guidance requires the prioritised topics to be placed on a materiality matrix, though the matrix in the report can be indicative.

Why GRI? Why not do your own thing? Or use another framework? A common chant from companies is 'we want a common consistent set of metrics that enables all companies to be compared like for like'. Ninety-four percent of the top Fortune 500 produce a sustainability report. KPMG's Survey on Corporate Reporting 2017 confirms that over 80% of large companies in 90 countries report using GRI. In addition, the use of other frameworks or self-made reporting lacks credibilty amongst stakeholders and investors. In addition, the view of many stock exchanges, governments and, of course, companies is that GRI is the leading and most highly respected de facto global standard for sustainability reporting. To positively impact reputation, use a respected reporting standard enabling common comparable and rankable metrics; GRI is the de facto gold standard.

Where is Food Waste disclosed? Food waste and material thrown away are an increasing concern Provisions to report food and other waste can be found at GRI 306.

11 Sustainability report evaluation

Once a basic understanding of the process to produce a report is known, it is good to reinforce knowledge by being able to evaluate reports. As time passes, stakeholders are becoming more adept at knowing the difference between PR and spin and a quality report, and this evaluation will make it even more difficult for companies to pull the proverbial wool over people's eyes.

During GRI-certified training masterclasses, the evaluation of reports is a light bulb moment. In the masterclass, the participants are asked to evaluate several reports; they look for certain pieces of information as well as provide a wider view on the reports they evaluate.

The exercise reveals real issues of content, quality and good practices. It also helps to crystallise what these report leaders will place in their own future reports, whether they are existing reporters or new reporters.

For many participants the value of the evaluation is instant for their organisation; they are able to take their existing or draft report and improve it there and then. They often review the processes they have used and are currently using, and have many ways to improve stakeholder engagement, determining what is material, and improve data collection and report writing, not to mention the benefit of managing and running organisations from MBA-level experienced sustainability and assurance experts.

Typical comments in the review session following the evaluation include:

- I now know what a good report should look like.
- I can now tell the difference between a good and not-so-good report.
- I am clearer on what reports are trying to say and where some succeed and others don't.
- I am clearer on how and why some organisations create a sense of trust, credibility and faith in the accuracy of their report.
- I can see the benefits of colour coding, infographics and so on in making reports more concise.

- I can see the importance of having a platform that delivers the whole report in one place.
- It is better for a report to tell a concise story that is easy to navigate; it is important to engagement and gathering interest from stakeholders.
- Cartoons and film are excellent as another content platform and perhaps more suited to PR and marketing where overindulgence in this area detracts from a main sustainability report.
- I can see how GRI harmonises with other standards and frameworks like CDP, OECD, IIRC, UN GC, PRI, UN Guiding Principles on Business and Human Rights and ISO.
- The evaluation is an excellent way to consolidate knowledge of producing good reports.
- GRI and sustainability reporting is demystified.

GRI positions some very clear requirements on what a report must contain. These are as follows:

> A sustainability report must contain a claim as a self-declaration on the 'in accordance' option, of either Core or Comprehensive. However, the GRI Standards seeks to be welcoming of organisations that are starting out or for whatever reason not quite at the Core option capacity to report, so GRI has the 'GRI-referenced' option (i.e. if the organisation does not reach the minimum criteria for Core, it cannot make the claim that its report has been prepared in accordance with the GRI Standards). In these cases, GRI-referenced is required to be included in any published materials identifying the specific social, economic and environmental disclosures, including the management approach which has been used.

The following two tables state the Disclosures. GRI requires a sustainability report to contain a claim that the report has been prepared in accordance with the GRI Standards 'Core' or 'Comprehensive' option.

The evaluation carries the reminder that a GRI report is not only about topics, but also the strategic, policy and procedural narrative on why the organisation reports, how it manages the material and how it evaluates the commitments to report that it makes. It is also about the reporting process, improvement and the decisions made. The report is not only a means of communication but also a tool for change and transformation. It is important to acknowledge that sustainability reporting is a living process that does not begin or end with a printed or online publication.

The evaluation is a systematic, documented, evidence-based methodology characterised by its focus on the process. It should be appreciated that

Disclosures	'In accordance' – Core (this information should be disclosed in all cases)	'In accordance' – Comprehensive (this information should be disclosed in all cases)
Organisational Profile	Disclosures 102–1 to 102–13	Disclosures 102–1 to 102–13
Strategy (directors' statement)	Disclosures 102–14	Disclosures 102–14 to 102–15
Ethics and Integrity	Disclosures 102–16	Disclosures 102–16 to 102–17
		Omissions allowed to 102–17
Governance	Disclosures 102–18	Disclosures 102–18 to 102–39
		Omissions allowed to 102–19 to 102–39
Stakeholder Engagement	Disclosures 102–40 to 102–44	Disclosures 102–40 to 102–44
Reporting Practice (including list of material topics and boundaries)	Disclosures 102–45 to 102–56	Disclosures 102–45 to 102–56
Disclosures from Sectors Disclosures	Optional, if available for the organisation's sector	Optional, if available for the organisation's sector

REQUIRED DISCLOSURES

Disclosures	'In accordance' – Core	'In accordance' – Comprehensive
101 Foundation	Applying the 10 Reporting Principles for Content and Quality	Applying the 10 Reporting Principles for Content and Quality
102 Standard Disclosures	33 Disclosures	56 Disclosures
103 Management Approach	Report on all material topics	Report on all material topics
	Omissions allowed to 103–2 and 103–3	Omissions allowed to 103–2 and 103–3
Topic-Specific Disclosures	There are 33 topics, 85 Disclosures	There are 33 topics, 85 Disclosures
200 Economic	At least one Disclosure related to each identified material topic	All Disclosures related to each identified material topic
300 Environmental		
400 Social		
Disclosures from Sectors Disclosures	Optional, if available for the organisation's sector	Optional, if available for the organisation's sector

any detailed consideration of the quality of the data in a report is the realms of assurance and auditors, and so outside the scope of this exercise.

Stakeholders should be able to directly access all of the report information from a single location. There is no minimum length for a report using the GRI Standards, as long as the organisation has properly applied the requirements of the standards.

The evaluation carries the reminder that reports should be written with discipline, the required areas should be easy to find in the first instance, and further meet with GRI's information expectations. The training test reviews reports for both these and specifically tests the information expectations of the report's content by asking participants a series of evaluation questions. The participant places their answers on a Sustainability Report Evaluation Questionnaire and a Score Matrix answer sheet provided. The report is scored from the answers provided on the Score Matrix. The beauty of this methodology is that it offers both the participants and trainers clear evidence as to whether they understand what a quality report should contain.

Next, we offer you a tool that will enable you to evaluate your own, or any, sustainability report.

Please remember that GRI uses specific terms in relation to its disclosures. 'Requirements' mean that the organisation 'shall' adhere to the directions of the disclosure. 'Recommendations' mean that the organisation 'should' adhere to the directions of the disclosure. And 'Guidance' denotes support for reporters to understand and apply the requirements and recommendations.

GRI-Certified Training Sustainability Report Evaluation – Scoring

Content – Stakeholder Inclusiveness – The reporting organisation shall identify its *stakeholders* and explain how it has responded to their reasonable expectations and interests.

1   **Yes/No** The reporting organisation can describe the stakeholders to whom it considers itself accountable;
2   **Yes/No** The report content draws upon the outcomes of stakeholder engagement processes used by the organisation in its ongoing activities and as required by the legal and institutional framework in which it operates;
3   **Yes/No** The report content draws upon the outcomes of any stakeholder engagement processes undertaken specifically for the report;
4   **Yes/No** The outcome of the stakeholder engagement processes that inform decisions about the report are consistent with the material topics included in the report.

Content – Sustainability Context – The report shall present the reporting organisation's performance in the wider context of *sustainability*.

1 **Yes/No** The reporting organisation presents its understanding of sustainable development, drawing on objective and available information and authoritative measures of sustainable development, for the topics covered;

2 **Yes/No** The organisation presents its performance with reference to broader sustainable development conditions and goals, as reflected in recognised sectoral, local, regional or global instruments;

3 **Yes/No** The organisation presents its performance in a manner that communicates its impacts and contributions in appropriate geographic contexts;

4 **Yes/No** The organisation describes how economic, environmental and/or social topics relate to its long-term strategy, risks, opportunities and goals, including in its value chain.

Content – Materiality – The report shall cover topics that:

- reflect the reporting organisation's significant economic, environmental and social *impacts*; or
- substantively influence the assessments and decisions of *stakeholders*.

1 **Yes/No** Reasonably estimable economic, environmental and/or social impacts (such as climate change, HIV/AIDS or poverty) identified through sound investigation by people with recognised expertise, or by expert bodies with recognised credentials;

2 **Yes/No** The interests and expectations of stakeholders specifically invested in the organisation, such as employees and shareholders;

3 **Yes/No** Broader economic, social and/or environmental interests and topics raised by stakeholders, such as workers who are not employees, suppliers, local communities, vulnerable groups and civil society;

4 **Yes/No** The main topics and future challenges for a sector, as identified by peers and competitors;

5 **Yes/No** Laws, regulations, international agreements or voluntary agreements of strategic significance to the organisation and its stakeholders;

6 **Yes/No** Key organisational values, policies, strategies, operational management systems, goals and targets;

7 **Yes/No** The core competencies of the organisation and the manner in which they can contribute to sustainable development;

8 **Yes/No** Consequences for the organisation that are related to its impacts on the economy, the environment and/or society (for example, risks to its business model or reputation);

9   **Yes/No** Material topics are appropriately prioritised in the report.

Content – Completeness – The report shall include coverage of *material topics* and their *boundaries*, sufficient to reflect significant economic, environmental and social *impacts*, and to enable *stakeholders* to assess the reporting organisation's performance in the *reporting period.*

1   **Yes/No** The report takes into account impacts the reporting organisation causes, contributes to or is directly linked to through a business relationship, and covers and prioritises all material information on the basis of the principles of materiality, sustainability context and stakeholder inclusiveness;
2   **Yes/No** The information in the report includes all significant impacts in the reporting period and reasonable estimates of significant future impacts when those impacts are reasonably foreseeable and can become unavoidable or irreversible;
3   **Yes/No** The report does not omit relevant information that substantively influences stakeholder assessments and decisions, or that reflects significant economic, environmental and social impacts.

Defining Report Quality – Accuracy – The reported information shall be sufficiently accurate and detailed for stakeholders to assess the reporting organisation's performance.

1   **Yes/No** The report indicates the data that has been measured;
2   **Yes/No** The measurements for data, and the basis for calculations, are adequately described and can be replicated with similar results;
3   **Yes/No** The margin of error for quantitative data is not sufficient to influence substantially the ability of stakeholders to reach appropriate and informed conclusions;
4   **Yes/No** The report indicates which data have been estimated, and the underlying assumptions and techniques used for the estimation, or where that information can be found;
5   **Yes/No** The qualitative statements in the report are consistent with other reported information and other available evidence.

Defining Report Quality – Balance – The reported information shall reflect positive and negative topics of the reporting organisation's performance to enable a reasoned assessment of overall performance.

1   **Yes/No** The report covers both favourable and unfavourable results and topics;

2   **Yes/No** The information in the report is presented in a format that allows users to see positive and negative trends in performance on a year-to-year basis;

3   **Yes/No** The emphasis on the various topics in the report reflects their relative priority.

Defining Report Quality – Clarity – The reporting organisation shall make information available in a manner that is understandable and accessible to stakeholders using that information.

1   **Yes/No** The report contains the level of information required by stakeholders but avoids excessive and unnecessary details;

2   **Yes/No** Stakeholders can find the specific information they want without unreasonable effort through tables of contents, maps, links or other aids;

3   **Yes/No** The report avoids technical terms, acronyms, jargon or other content likely to be unfamiliar to stakeholders, and includes explanations (where necessary) in the relevant section or in a glossary;

4   **Yes/No** The information in the report is available to stakeholders, including those with particular accessibility needs, such as differing abilities, language or technology.

Defining Report Quality – Comparability – The reporting organisation shall select, compile and report information consistently. The reported information shall be presented in a manner that enables stakeholders to analyse changes in the organisation's performance over time and that could support an analysis relative to other organisations.

1   **Yes/No** The report and its information can be compared on a year-to-year basis;

2   **Yes/No** The reporting organisation's performance can be compared with appropriate benchmarks;

3   **Yes/No** Any significant variation between reporting periods in the list of material topics, topic boundaries, length of reporting period or information covered in the report can be identified and explained;

4   **Yes/No** When they are available, the report utilises generally accepted protocols for compiling, measuring and presenting information, including the information required by the GRI Standards.

Defining Report Quality – Reliability – The reporting organisation shall gather, record, compile, analyse and report information and processes used in the preparation of the report in a way in which they can be subject to examination and which establishes the quality and materiality of the information.

1 **Yes/No** The scope and extent of external assurance is identified;
2 **Yes/No** The organisation can identify the original sources of the information in the report;
3 **Yes/No** The organisation can provide reliable evidence to support assumptions or complex calculations;
4 **Yes/No** Representation is available from the original data or information owners, attesting to its accuracy within acceptable margins of error.

Defining Report Quality – Timeliness – The reporting organisation shall report on a regular schedule so that information is available in time for stakeholders to make informed decisions.

1 **Yes/No** Information in the report has been disclosed while it is recent, relative to the reporting period;
2 **Yes/No** The information in the report clearly indicates the time period to which it relates, when it will be updated and when the latest updates were made, and separately identifies any restatements of previous disclosures along with the reasons for restatement.

Management Approach – The reporting organisation shall provide an explanation of why the topic is material, which can include: a description of the significant impacts identified and the reasonable expectations and interests of stakeholders regarding the topic; a description of the process, such as due diligence, that the organisation used to identify the impacts related to the topic; the boundary for the material topic and evaluation of the organisation's management approach.

1 **Yes/No** For each material topic, the report contains an explanation of why the topic is material and the boundary for each material topic;
2 **Yes/No** For each material topic, the report contains an explanation of how the organisation manages the topic with a statement of the purpose of the management approach and the polices, commitments, goals and target, responsibilities resources, and so on (see GRI 103–2);
3 **Yes/No** For each material topic, the report contains an explanation of how the organisation evaluates the management approach, including the mechanism for evaluating, the results and any related adjustments.

SCHEDULE 1 – MATRIX

1   Scoring method used to do evaluation, ✓/✗/? (see example provided).
Use a format such as Schedule 1 to provide responses for compliance (✓),
unknown (?) or non-compliance (✗) for each set question, coupled with an
area to make observations and constructive commentary about performance.

MATRIX FOR END-OF-COURSE SR EVALUATION

Sustainability Report Evaluation Questionnaire – Schedule 1

KEY: ✗**Non-compliant**   **?Not Clear**   ✓**Compliant**

Example

Materiality (9)											Score	Observations
	✓	✓	✓	✓	✗	✗	✗	✓	?		5	*Really effective matrix*

Report Areas	Question Numbers										Score (Total's)	Observations/ Notes
	1	2	3	4	5	6	7	8	9	10		
Stakeholder Inclusiveness (4)												
Sustainability Context (4)												
Materiality (9)												
Completeness (3)												
Accuracy (5)												
Balance (3)												
Clarity (4)												
Comparability (4)												
Reliability (4)												
Timeliness (2)												
Management Approach (3)												
Total												

Appendix 1

The usual suspects – an idea of material topics and challenges for organisations in different sectors

When we give talks on sustainability, in the initial conversations with organisations they will often ask, 'What are the main material matters, impacts and challenges for my industry?'

Identifying what we call 'The Usual Suspects' (i.e. 'The Usual Material Topics') can be very helpful and illuminating to organisations as a rapid bench-marking exercise. It has instant value to both calibrate an organisation's existing reporting machinery, and as a means of new reporters forming ideas to kickstart the task of preparing to report. It can also be used to start discussion at various stages of the journey: initial governance approval to start reporting, executive meeting discussions, gathering the sustainability team discussion, kick-off meeting discussions, Prepare phase, stakeholder discussions, Connect phase, defining material topics discussion and the Define phase.

The main challenges in different sectors are as follows:

Event Companies – Sourcing food, beverages and equipment, legacy, transport by attendees, Food Waste, Plastics Waste, fines for noncompliance – Event Organisers Sector Disclosure

Media – Platforms, content, emissions, conservation through communications – Media Sector Disclosure

Banks – Infrastructure investments pro bono, fines for noncompliance, financial services access for the disadvantaged, training and education, marketing communications – Finance Sector Disclosure

Multinational Food Company – Fair labour, human rights, environmental waste from factories, food waste, plastic waste from packaging, occupational health and Safety, customer health and safety – Food Processing Sector Disclosure

Multinational Retail and Food Company – Energy, emissions, food waste, plastic waste from packaging, supply chain impact and support for ethics and training, product responsibility through sustainable sourcing and healthy living

Multinational Oil Company – Emissions (BP has a business case carbon price), effluents and spills, H&S concerns for staff, and (dare we say it) support from governments that expend large sums on lobbying – Oil and Gas Sector Disclosure

Mulinational Drinks Company – Product responsibility concerns, fair labour and human rights, environmental waste from factories, occupational health and Safety, customer health and safety

Medium-Sized Electronics Company – Fair labour and human rights, environmental waste from factories, H&S concerns for staff and in regard to the products, supply chain (conflict minerals matters)

National-Sized Construction Company – Emissions, materials used, waste, occupational health and Safety, and increasingly legacy (long-term benefits to communities). Corruption, procurement and product standards (the gap between design and construction outcomes), supply chain practice, plus gender diversity and equality of opportunity as long-established problems – Construction and Real Estate Sector Disclosure

International NGO – The main sustainability challenges are connected to public policy positions, project operations including indirect economic impacts in local communities, emissions related to expatriate project staff travel, effluents and waste, non-discrimination, workforce by type, training and education, fines for noncompliance – NGO Sector Disclosure

Medium-Sized Apparel Company – Fair labour/wages and human rights, environmental and material waste from factories, and H&S risks

SME Sustainability Consultancy – Product responsibility, emissions, economic performance, training and education, in-kind pro bono service support, maintaining certifications as a license to operate, improving skills to maintain relevance to customers

Local City Council – The main sustainability challenges are engagement in sustainability initiatives, pollution/waste management and fair labour/wage risks

Micro Company (like a local guest house) – concerned with labour conditions, impacts on their local communities, and customer health and safety

But remember, don't let individuals or experts tell you what is best to report on because the proper way is to be guided by stakeholders. Experts disagree as to the important Topics – in Asia and Africa, companies cite labour standards and human rights as most material, whereas in Europe and North America disclosures on carbon emissions are at the top of the agenda.

Some commentators suggest that SMEs find systematically working through the GRI requirements easier to implement than larger organisations because they are closer to their staff and business activities. They often work on a first-name basis with their supply chain. As a sustainability consultancy supporting and guiding organisation, we see the key issues as being leadership and people management to embed integrated approaches and good supply chain relationships by thoroughly sharing information on impacts.

Glossary

A

Air pollution: Air is made up of a number of gases, mostly nitrogen and oxygen and, in smaller amounts, water vapour, carbon dioxide, argon and other trace gases. Air pollution occurs when harmful chemicals and particles are emitted into the air – due to human activity or natural forces – at a concentration that interferes with human health or welfare or that harms the environment in other ways.

Assurance: GRI recommends competent assurance at GRI Standards.33 from independent professional assurance providers competent in GRI and the sector in question. However, GRI does not make assurance a requirement. Type 1 Assurance will only assess the reporting principle: materiality, stakeholder inclusivity and responsiveness. Type 2 Assurance is better because it looks at the data. The level of detail for the assurance will be either 'Moderate', requiring specific evidence per material item, or 'High', requiring a thorough assessment of the information, people and reporting processes and data at many of the organisation's installations across the world.

Audit: Systematic examination or verification of an organisation's books of account against specific criteria by qualified accountants, such as accounting standards in the case of a financial statement audit or organisational policies and procedures in the case of an internal audit.

B

Biodiversity: A short form of the phrase 'biological diversity', which means the variety of life on this planet and how it interacts within habitats and ecosystems. Biodiversity covers all plants, animals and micro-organisms on land and in water. See also Ecosystem; Habitat; Organism.

Boundaries: Direct and indirect contributions of an organisation to the day-to-day impacts of its material topics.

Business model: There is no single, generally accepted definition of the term 'business model'. However, it is often seen as the process by which an organisation seeks to create and sustain value. It is dependent upon internal and external parameters, the availability, affordability, quality and management of various resources, or 'capital' (financial, manufactured, human, intellectual, natural and social).

C

Capital: The resources and relationships that support the long-term viability of an organisation, such as:

Financial capital – The pool of funds that is available to the organisation for use in the production of goods or the provision of services, and obtained through financing, such as debt, equity or grants, or generated through operations or investments.

Manufactured capital – Manufactured physical objects (as distinct from natural physical objects) that are available to the organisation for use in the production of goods or the provision of services, including: buildings, equipment and infrastructure (such as roads, ports, bridges and waste and water treatment plants).

Human capital – People's skills and experience, and their motivations to innovate, including their alignment with and support of the organisation's governance framework and ethical values such as its recognition of human rights; their ability to understand and implement an organisation's strategies; and their loyalties and motivations for improving processes, goods and services, including their ability to lead and to collaborate.

Intellectual capital – Intangibles that provide competitive advantage, including: intellectual property, such as patents, copyrights, software and organisational systems, procedures and protocols; and the intangibles that are associated with the brand and reputation that an organisation has developed.

Natural capital – An input to the production of goods or the provision of services, including water, land, minerals and forests; and biodiversity and eco-system health. An organisation's activities also impact, positively or negatively, on natural capital and social capital.

Social capital – The institutions and relationships established within and between each community, group of stakeholders and other networks to enhance individual and collective well-being, including common values and behaviours; key relationships, and the trust and loyalty that an organisation has developed and strives to build and protect with customers, suppliers and business partners; and an organisation's social license to operate.

Capital allocation: A process of how an organisation divides its financial resources and other sources of capital between different processes, people and projects. Overall, it is management's goal to optimise capital allocation so that it generates as much wealth as possible for its shareholders.

Carbon emissions: In the context of climate change, carbon dioxide is released when substances, especially oil, gas and coal, are burned by vehicles and planes, by factories and by homes.

Carbon footprint: A measure of the impact our activities have on the environment, especially climate change, often reported as the units of tonnes (or kg) of carbon dioxide each of us produces over a given period of time.

Carbon offset: A unit, equal to one ton of carbon dioxide that individuals, companies or governments buy to reduce short-term and long-term emissions of greenhouse gases. The payment usually funds projects that generate energy from renewable sources, such as wind or flowing water. Individuals can choose whether to buy an offset (for example, to compensate for air travel), but governments and large industries are sometimes required to buy them to meet international targets aimed at reducing greenhouse gases.

Climate: The pattern of weather in a particular region over a set period of time, usually 30 years. The pattern is affected by the amount of rain or snowfall, average temperatures throughout the year, humidity, wind speeds and so on. The UK has a temperate climate, in which it doesn't get too hot or too cold.

Climate change: A change in the climate of a region over time due to natural forces or human activity. In the context of the UN Framework Convention on Climate Change, it is the change in climate caused by higher levels of greenhouse gases in the atmosphere due to human activities as well as natural climate changes. See also Global warming; UN Framework Convention on Climate Change.

Comparability: The quality or state of being similar or alike.

Connectivity: The connection between the different components of the organisation's business model, external factors that affect the organisation and the various resources and relationships on which the organisation and its performance depend. Connectivity of information is one of the Guiding Principles.

Content elements: Key items that are included and interconnected in an integrated report based on the application of the Guiding Principles. The content elements identified in the discussion paper are as follows:

Organisational overview and business model
Operating context, including risks and opportunities

Strategic objectives and strategies to achieve those objectives
Governance and remuneration
Performance
Future outlook

E

Ecosystem: A community of organisms that depend on each other and the environment they inhabit.

Emissions: In the context of the atmosphere, gases or particles released into the air that can contribute to global warming or poor air quality.

Emissions trading allowance: Permission to emit to the atmosphere one tonne of carbon dioxide equivalent during a specific trading period. The allowance is only valid for the purpose of the directive and can only be transferred in accordance with the directive.

ESG: A term used to refer to environmental, social and governance (ESG) factors, particularly in the context of financial markets and investment decision-making.

External factors: Facts or situations from outside the organisation which influence or impact the organisation. External factors may be characterised as economic conditions, societal issues and technological changes.

F

Footprint: Impacts of an organisation that extend beyond its reporting boundary, which in an integrated report would include major external economic, environmental and social impacts up and down the supply chain.

Future orientation: One of the Guiding Principles for preparation of an integrated report to include management's expectations about the future, as well as other information to help users report, understand and assess the organisation's prospects and the uncertainties it faces.

G

Global warming: The gradual increase in temperature of the Earth's surface caused by human activities that cause high levels of carbon dioxide and other gases to be released into the air.

Governance: Establishment of policies, and continuous monitoring of their proper implementation, by the members of the governing body of an organisation. It includes the mechanisms required to balance the powers of the members (with the associated accountability), and their primary duty of enhancing the prosperity and viability of the organisation.

Greenhouse effect: The warming of the Earth's atmosphere caused by increasing levels of gases, such as water vapour and carbon dioxide. These gases absorb radiation emitted naturally from the ground and therefore slow down the loss of energy from the Earth. The greenhouse effect has always existed; without it, Earth would be too cold for plants, animals and people to survive. But because of the increase in greenhouse gas emissions in recent years, the greenhouse effect is a lot stronger, leading to global warming. See also Global warming; Greenhouse gases; Radiation.

Greenhouse gases: Gases such as carbon dioxide and methane which tend to trap heat radiating from the Earth's surface, causing warming in the lower atmosphere. The major greenhouse gases that cause climate change are carbon dioxide (CO_2), methane (CH_4) and nitrous oxide (NO_2). See also Greenhouse effect; Global warming.

GRI reporting options: In accordance with the GRI Standards 'Core' or 'Comprehensive' options, or GRI Referenced.

Guiding Principles: Concepts that describe the outcomes that an integrated report should achieve and that guide decisions made throughout the integrated reporting process. The Guiding Principles proposed in the discussion paper include:

Strategic focus
Connectivity of information
Future orientation
Responsiveness and stakeholder inclusiveness
Conciseness, reliability and materiality

I

Impacts: Measure of the tangible and intangible effects (consequences) of an external factor on the organisation and of the organisation's actions or influence upon another.

Inclusivity: See Stakeholder engagement.

Integrated report: A single report that provides a clear and concise representation of how an organisation demonstrates stewardship and how it creates and sustains value.

Integrated reporting: A process that brings together material information about an organisation's strategy, governance, performance and prospects in a way that reflects the commercial, social and environmental context within which it operates.

Integrated Reporting Framework: A framework to guide organisations on communicating the broad set of information needed by investors and other stakeholders to assess the organisation's long-term prospects in a clear, concise, connected and comparable format.

Integrated thinking: Application of the collective mind of those charged with governance and the ability of management to monitor, manage and communicate the full complexity of the value-creation process and how this contributes to success over time; may also be referred to as integrated management.

Interdependency: A dynamic of being mutually and physically responsible to, and sharing a common set of relationships with many others, such as between strategy and risk, financial and nonfinancial performance, governance and performance, and between the organisation's own performance and that of others in its value chain.

International Integrated Reporting Framework: A framework for integrated reporting to be developed by the International Integrated Reporting Committee that would be international in scope.

Investors: The owner(s) of a financial asset, including capital stock and debt.

K

Key performance topics (KPIs):   A set of quantifiable measures used to assess an organisation's performance in critical areas.

Key risk topics (KRIs):   The topics by which key risks (those which the organisation perceives to be its most significant risks) can be easily identified and managed.

M

Mainstream report: The primary reporting vehicle.

Management commentary: A narrative description by the organisation to provide insights into its performance. Management commentary may be required in particular jurisdictions or prepared voluntarily. Frameworks for management commentary may be established by regulation or be developed by others (e.g. a broad, non-binding framework for the presentation of management commentary that relates to financial statements prepared in accordance with International Financial Reporting Standards [IFRSs] has been issued by the International Accounting Standards Board).

Materiality: A matter is material if it will influence the decisions, actions or performance of an individual or an organisation. In a financial reporting context, a matter is material if it would be likely to influence investment decisions made by current or prospective shareholders.

In the context of sustainability reporting, the concept is extended to incorporate environmental, social or economic factors relevant and significant to the organisation and its stakeholders.

N

Non-financial information: Information regarding an organisation's performance measured in terms other than financial (e.g. sustainability measurements). Such measurements may be in quantitative or qualitative terms.

O

Opportunities: An occasion or situation which makes it possible for an organisation to do something that it wants to do or has to do, or the possibility of doing something.

Outcomes: Intangible results of an activity, plan, process or program. In an integrated report, it also includes the action(s) taken through the analysis or comparison with the intended or projected results.

Outputs: Quantifiable or tangible results of an activity, effort or process; often an output can be expressed in numbers (quantitatively measured).

P

Performance: Qualitative and quantitative information about how the organisation has performed against its strategic objectives and related strategies.

R

Reforestation: The process of planting trees in forest lands to replace those that have been cut down.

Relevance: Pertinence (relation) to the matter at hand. In an integrated report, relevance is considered in relation to the organisation's reporting boundary and footprint, and the content elements.

Reporting boundary: In GRI, it forms the basis of an organisation's contribution to the cause of the impact; it clarifies whether the contribution is direct, indirect or both. The boundary for an integrated report refers to the range of entities whose performance is covered in the organisation's financial statements.

Reporting option: In accordance with GRI Standards 'Core' or 'Comprehensive' options.

Remuneration: The total compensation received by an executive, which includes not only the base salary but options, bonuses, expense accounts and other forms of compensation.

Renewable energy: Energy from renewable resources such as wind power, solar energy or biomass.

Renewable resource: A resource that can be used again and again without reducing its supply because it is constantly topped up, for example wind or sun rays.

Reporting instruments: Any instrument, voluntary or mandatory, that requires or encourages organisations to report their sustainability performance. There are nearly 400 across the world, such as Carrots and Sticks.

Resources and relationships: See Capital.

Responsiveness: Quick to act, especially to meet the needs of someone (e.g. a stakeholder) or something (e.g. a regulation).

Risk: The potential that a chosen action or activity (including the choice of inaction) will lead to a loss (an undesirable outcome).

S

Sector disclosures: There are ten Sector Disclosures accessed from GRI's website. Sector Disclosures are defined as tailored versions of the GRI Standards. They are available for the sectors of, Construction and Real Estate, Oil and Gas, Mining, Airports Operator, Media, Food Processing, Events, Financial Services, Electric Utilities, and NGO's.

Stakeholder: A person, group or organisation that can affect or be affected by an organisation's actions, objectives or policies. Stakeholders in a business organisation may include creditors, customers, directors, employees, governments, shareholders, suppliers, unions and the community from which the organisation draws its resources.

Stakeholder engagement: An activity that an organisation uses to help it identify and respond to significant concerns of a variety of stakeholders and thereby achieve inclusivity.

Stewardship: The responsibility for taking good care of resources entrusted to the organisation.

Strategic objective: Ultimate objective that an organisation is striving to achieve through its strategies.

Strategies: The pattern of decisions and actions that are taken by an organisation to achieve its strategic objectives.

Supply chain: The system of organisations, people, technology, activities, information and resources involved in delivering a product or service.

Sustainability: Actions and approaches adopted by an organisation compatible with, and contributing to, organisational resilience and sustainable development.

Sustainability report: A report produced by an organisation on its economic, environmental and social impacts (positive and negative) of its day-to-day activities.

Sustainable development: Development using land or energy sources in a way that meets the needs of people today without compromising the ability of future generations to meet their own needs.

Sustainable Development Goals: Sustainable Development Goals are part of the UN Global Policy the UN 2030 Agenda for Sustainable Development.

V

Value chain: The high-level interrelationship between an organisation's key operations or activities (including upstream activities) that are involved in delivering value to that business' customers.

Value creation: A mechanism which converts financial and non-financial inputs to certain outputs including financial performance. It is influenced by external factors that present risks and opportunities, which create the context within which an organisation operates, co-created through relationships with others, and dependent on the availability, affordability, quality and management of various resources, or 'capital'.

Z

Zero emissions: An engine, motor or other energy source that does not produce any gas or release any harmful gases directly into the environment.

Bibliography

Corporate Register CR Perspectives 2013 www.csr-reporting.blogspot.co.il/2013/11/csr-time-for-some-perspective.html

Gbangbola, Kye Basic Reporting CM. April 2012

Gbangbola, Kye GRI Measurement and Reporting How to Do It and the Benefits http://construction-manager.co.uk/construction-professional/measuring-carbon-challenge/

Gbangbola, Kye GRI Standards Selection Tool – Latest GRI Guidance on Sustainability Reporting and Its Focus on Materiality. *2013 Environmentalist Journal.* October 2013, pages 31–32 www.environmentalistonline.com/article/2013-10-07/sustainability-report-selection-tool

Gbangbola, Kye Guardian Article on GRI Standards Calming the Situation Down http://aheadahead.wordpress.com/category/blogs-in-guardian-sustainability-business/

Gbangbola, Kye How to Do GRI www.totalecomanagement.co.uk/events.html

Gbangbola, Kye Is Your Radar On? Sustainability Is Not an Ideology, It Is a Necessity. December 12 www.cbcschemes.org.uk/sites/cbcschemes.org.uk/files/cbc_review_magazine_-_issue_7_dec_12.pdf

Gbangbola, Kye International Integrated Reporting Pilot – Achieving Construction Excellence Through Corporate Reporting www.carbonaction2050.com/sites/carbonaction2050.com/files/document-attachment/Kye%20Gbangbola%2003.11.11.doc

Gbangbola, Kye Leadership and Corporate Activity June 2013 www.buildup.eu/publications/23282

Gbangbola, Kye Measuring Up to the Carbon Challenge April 2011 www.construction-manager.co.uk//construction-professional/measuring-carbon-challenge/

Gbangbola, Kye New Reforms Strengthen Non-Financial Reporting in the UK www.totalecomanagement.co.uk/news-resources.html

Gbangbola, Kye Quick Introduction to GRI Standards. May 2013 www.totalecomanagement.co.uk/news-resources.html

Gbangbola, Kye Sustainable Development and the London Olympics. December 2012 www.totalecomanagement.co.uk/events.html

Gbangbola, Kye Transform Magazine Sustainability and Disability into the Fold – A Unique Article Setting Out the Issues and Best Practice to Achieve Equality for Disabled People in the Sustainability Sector and Working World https://transform.iema.net/article/fold-changing-attitudes-towards-disability-workplace

The Girl Who Silenced the World 'You Are What You Do, Not What You Say' www. youtube.com/watch?v=TQmz6Rbpnu0

Global Reporting Initiative GRI www.globalreporting.org

International Integrated Reporting Initiative IIRC www.theiirc.org

KPMG Survey of Corporate Responsibility Reporting 2017 https://home.kpmg.com/ xx/en/home/campaigns/2017/10/survey-of-corporate-responsibility-reporting-2017. html

Marks & Spencer PLC 2013 Sustainability Report http://static.globalreporting.org/ report-pdfs/2013/04908206daa5134592515ee4e319d1c4.pdf

The 'Story of Stuff' 'You Can't Run a Liner System on a Finite Planet Indefinitely' www.youtube.com/watch?v=9GorqroigqMandRio+20

The US Green Economy by Professor Mark Maslin, (UCL Geography) UCL News. https://www.ucl.ac.uk/news/2019/oct/us-green-economy-worth-13-trillion-year

United Nations Resolution 'Towards Global Partnerships' United Nations General Assembly 2013 A/C.2/68/L.24 www.unglobalcompact.org/docs/about_the_gc/ government_support/A_C.2_68_L.24.pdf

Index

Note: Page numbers in *italics* indicate figures and page numbers in **bold** indicate tables on the corresponding pages.

Accountability AA1000AS Standard 68
assurance: Accountability AA1000AS Standard in 68; credibility and 67–68; GRI standards in 69; teams for 68
Attenborough, D. 1

business case for reporting 12–17
Byanyima, W. 6

CEO/senior person's narrative 56
checking services, GRI 61–62
climate change 5
company accreditations 56–57
Connect phase: building stakeholder relationships in 37; identification of stakeholders in 29–30, *30*; prioritisation of stakeholders in 30–31, **32**; stakeholder engagement in 31–35, *33*; timeline of 28–29, 40
conservation efforts 6
Content Index 57–58, *59–60*, 76
context, sustainability 4–7
Core and Comprehensive Option 21–24, **23**, 76, 78
Corporate Social Responsibility 1
CRAB TC 7, 21, 45–47
Critical Path Programe (CPA) 12

Define phase: determining material topics in 40–42; producing materiality matrix and determining 'thresholds' in 42–43; timeline of 38–40; validating material topics in 43–44
Development Plan 24
diversity impact of reporting process 16
Dow Jones Group 3

Eco Team 8
engagement of stakeholders 31–35, *33*
environmental/sustainability matters in reporting process 16
European Non-Financial Reporting Directive 3
evaluation, sustainability report: components of 78–80; GRI-certified training sustainability report evaluation scoring 80–84; matrix for 85; typical questions in 77–78
Extinction Rebellion 1

feedback, report 64
financial implications of reporting process 14–15, 75

Global Green Economy 4
GRI Sustainability Disclosure Database 22
GRI sustainability reporting: assurance 67–69; benefits of 75, 76; board approval and preparing the business case in 12–17; Connect phase of (*see* Connect phase); costs of 75; Define phase of (*see* Define phase); examples of 75; good and bad

74–75; integrated reporting 70–73; knowledge needed for 74; mandatory 75–76; on metrics measurement 14; Monitor phase of (*see* Monitor phase); origins of 74; preliminaries in 8–12, *9–11*; Prepare phase of (*see* Prepare phase); principles of 4–5; process in 17–19; as public good 14; questions and answers about 74–76; report evaluation in 77–85; report writing in (*see* report writing); Sustainability Reporting Tool (SRT) software for 65–66; Sustainable Development Goals (SDGs) and 7–8; timeline *9–11*; understanding standards of 21–24, **23**

human resource and establishment matters in reporting process 15

identification of stakeholders 29–30, *30* 'in accordance' option in GRI standards 21–24, **23**
integrated reporting 70–73
Intergovernmental Climate Change Panel 4
International Energy Agency (IEA) 5
International Integrated Reporting Council (IIRC) 71–73
International Reporting (IR) Framework 70–73

kick-off meeting 25–27, *27*
KPMG International Survey of Corporate Sustainability 49, 67; Reporting 2–3, 40

London Olympic Games 41

mandatory reporting 75–76
materiality: determination of 40–42; matrix and thresholds of 42–43; usual suspects for 86–88; validation of 43–44
Millennium Development Goals 5
Monitor phase: monitoring topics and setting policies and procedures to measure as necessary in 47–49, **48**; setting SMART goals and targets in 49–51, **50**; timeline of 45–47

National Adaptation Programme (NAP), UK 5

omissions, report 58, 61
Oxfam 6

policies and procedures for monitoring topics 47–49, **48**
pollution 5, 6
population growth 6
Prepare phase: assembling the team in 20–21; Development Plan in 24; kick-off meeting in 25–27, *27*; timeline of 20; understanding GRI standards and choosing the 'in accordance' option in 21–24, **23**
prioritising of stakeholders 30–31, **32**
programme of works in reporting process 14
proposal in reporting process 13–14
publication, report 63

quality of GRI sustainability reporting 74–75

recommendations in reporting process 16
report writing: claim made in 57; company accreditations in 56–57; content index 57–58, *59–60*; contents and layout of report in 54–56; developing narrative for most senior person's statement in 56; draft sustainability/integrated report 57; evaluation of 77–85; examples of 75; feedback on 64; finalising and sending for publication in 63; GRI report-checking services and 61–62; omissions in 58, 61; report launch after 63; timeline of 52–54
risks in reporting process 15–16

SMART goals and targets 8, 49–51, **50**
software, Sustainability Reporting Tool (SRT) 65–66
stakeholders 4–7; assurance and 69; building relationships with 37; communication methods and 52; Connect phase timeline for 28–29,

40; difficulties with participation by 16; engagement of 31–35, *33*; feedback from 64; identifying 29–30, *30*; prioritising 30–31, **32**
sustainability leader and coordinator role 8, 12; in identifying stakeholders 29–30
sustainability reporting 1–3; mandatory 75–76; *see also* GRI sustainability reporting
Sustainability Reporting Tool (SRT) software 65–66
Sustainable Development Goals (SDGs) 7–8

Thunberg, G. 1

United Nations (UN) 1, 4; Sustainability Development Goals (SDGs) 7–8

validation of material topics 43–44

waste management 5–6
water pollution 5
wealth distribution 6
World Bank 5
World Economic Forum 6
World Health Organisation (WHO) 6
World Wildlife Fund 4

Printed in the United States
by Baker & Taylor Publisher Services

.